VINYL

Haynes

How to get the best from your vinyl records and kit

First published in November 2017

A catalogue record for this book is available from the British Library.

ISBN 978 1 78521 165 2

Library of Congress control no. 2017949616

Published by Haynes Publishing,
Sparkford, Yeovil, Somerset BA22 7JJ, UK.
Tel: 01963 440635
Int. tel: +44 1963 440635
Website: www.haynes.com

Haynes North America Inc.,
859 Lawrence Drive, Newbury Park,
California 91320, USA.

Printed in Malaysia.

Matt Anniss

A fanatical vinyl hoarder since the age of 12, Matt Anniss has spent the last two decades writing about music and DJ culture. Since editing *IDJ* magazine in the mid-2000s, he has written for *Red Bull Music Academy Daily*, *Mixmag*, *Resident Advisor* and *Juno Plus*. His book credits include numerous titles on music and DJ culture for children and young adults. He lives in Bristol with a 10,000-strong record collection.

Patrick Fuller

Patrick's extensive vinyl collection went missing shortly after he left home in 1987. Happily, it turned up 15 years later in his brother's friend's attic, complete with 1,000 rock, pop, classical and dance records the Fuller family had mislaid over the years. Patrick, a former journalist and editor, now plays the records (and many more acquired since) on his beloved Technics SL1210s given to him by his wife Louise. His six children have given up complaining.

Acknowledgements

The author and editor would like to thank the following for their assistance during the production of this book:

The team at What Hi-Fi? Sound and Vision: Alastair Lewis, Claire Griffiths, Simon Bowles, Simon Lucas, Andy Clough and Sarah Hunt; Audio Technica; Oli Ackroyd (Scratch Pro Audio); Chris Cooper, Chris Farrell (Idle Hands); Hugo Fuller; Andrew Golby (Haynes PLC); GZ Media; Ned Hawes, Jake Holloway & Zaf Chowdhry (LoveVinyl); Markus Holler (Sugarbush Records); Shawn Joseph (Optimum Mastering); Lol Lecanu (Richer Sounds); Richard Marshall (Boogie Nights); Gareth Morgan, Paul Morrissey (Bozak); Paul Murphy & Simon Purnell (Claremont 56); Mike Savage (Prime Cuts); Louise, who provided the ultimate inspiration: my SL1210s.

VINYL

How to get the best from your vinyl records and kit

Owners' Workshop Manual

188 pages of vinyl tech and technique, with hints and tips
from the world's top professionals

Matt Anniss & Patrick Fuller

Contents

→ **Pro-Ject's VTE is a rare vertical-mount turntable, where the vinyl is clamped in and stands on its end. It is belt drive and can be wall mounted** *(Henley Audio)*

Introduction

At the turn of the millennium, it appeared that the days of vinyl records were numbered. Yet seventeen years into the 2000s, sales of records continue to rise at a rapid rate. In 2016, over 13 million new vinyl albums and singles were sold in the United States alone – a ten per cent increase on the previous year. In the UK it was 3.2 million, up 53 per cent, with David Bowie's Blackstar the biggest seller. No one quite knows how many secondhand records are swapping hands at the same time, but it is likely to be hundreds of millions.

For those passionate about music, there is simply no finer medium than vinyl, the ultimate expression of 'tangible music'. While arguments about whether records sound better than digital will continue to rage for ever, there's no denying that the experience of buying, collecting and playing vinyl is far more satisfying than streaming tracks on your smartphone.

For some, vinyl is not so much a music storage medium as a way of life. They spend inordinate amounts of time tweaking their home hi-fi set-up in a bid to get the finest possible sound reproduction, devote their weekends to record shopping expeditions and obsess over the minute details of each and every album or single they own.

If you are not already one of these people, then sooner or later you will be. Buying this book is your first step on the road to vinyl addiction.

We hope you enjoy reading it. Like the building of a brilliant record collection or the design of a mind-blowing turntable, it was a genuine labour of love.

Matt Anniss and Patrick Fuller

Chapter One

The Record Players

The story of the record player

A potted history of turntables and record players, from the pioneering sound recorders of the 1860s to the present day.

The origins of the tried-and-tested turntable can be traced back to 1853, and the moment a Parisian printer began proofreading a set of etchings destined for a physics textbook.

As Edouard-Leon Scott de Martinville worked his way though the illustrations, he came across an anatomical drawing of the inside of the human ear. The Frenchman began to wonder whether it would be possible to create a mechanical device based on the workings of the ear that could successfully record sound.

In 1857, Scott de Martinville unveiled his 'mechanical ear', patented as the 'phonautograph'. The groundbreaking machine used a horn to collect sound, which was then passed through an elastic membrane attached to a stylus. This rudimentary 'needle' created an impression on smoke-blackened paper or glass, effectively recording sound as a visual waveform. In 2008, scientists successfully turned Scott de Martinville's primitive etchings of sound waves into actual sounds: 20-second snatches of the inventor singing French folk song 'Au Claire de la Lune'.

Sing it back

Scott de Martinville's breakthrough was remarkable, though he'd yet to work out how to play back recorded sounds. The first person to successfully tackle this issue was a fellow Frenchman, poet-turned-amateur-scientist Charles Cros.

In 1877, Cros lodged papers with the French Academy of Sciences proposing a method for playing back phonautograph recordings. Cros's system converted phonautograph tracings in soot into a groove or ridge on a metal disc. A stylus linked to a diaphragm would then 'ride the grooves', effectively reading the recorded vibrations. The diaphragm would transmit these vibrations into the air, effectively reproducing the original sound.

Cros's 'paleophone' was far-sighted and pioneering, but overlooked at the time of invention. He received little credit for his 'recorded disc' innovation. Instead, the world went crazy for a new machine from one of America's most prolific inventors, Thomas Edison.

← Publicity-hungry inventor Thomas Edison won praise for bringing the world the phonograph, the electrographic vote recorder, the carbon filament light bulb and the alkaline battery

The wizard gets to work

Thomas Edison had initially been trying to improve the efficiency of a telegraph transmitter when he got the idea for what would become the phonograph. During his research, the inventor noticed that if you played back telegraph tape at high speed, it gave off a noise resembling the human voice.

Edison began trying to record telephone calls by attaching a diaphragm and needle to the receiver. Like Scott de Martinville's earlier device, the stylus would make a mark in paper when someone spoke. His great breakthrough came when he covered a cylinder in tinfoil and used that as the recording medium. When he reversed the process, he was astonished to hear the words he'd spoken during the recording: 'Mary had a little lamb'.

Ever the showman, Edison decided to demonstrate his device to the editorial team at *Scientific American* magazine. The publication later recalled the encounter in an 1896 article: 'In December 1877, a young man came into the office and placed before the editors a small, simple machine about which very few preliminary remarks were offered. The visitor without any ceremony whatever turned the crank, and to the astonishment of all present the machine said: "Good morning. How do you do? How do you like the phonograph?" The machine thus spoke for itself.'

The machine was a revelation and led to Edison being dubbed 'The Wizard of Menlo

→ The graphophone was capable of producing superior sound to Edison's phonograph but was not as commercially successful *(Leslie J. Newville, Project Gutenberg)*

Park'. He was invited to demonstrate his device at the White House, where he made a recording of President Rutherford B. Hayes using his tinfoil-and-cylinder method. The recording survives to this day in Edison's artefacts, though is too fragile to play.

Wax and wane

On the back of Edison's invention, which was quickly turned from a prototype into a machine that America's well-off could purchase to amaze their friends, a gaggle of rival inventors created their own alternative systems. Chief among these was Alexander Graham Bell – of the telephone fame – whose Volta Laboratory spent five years developing the rival graphophone.

Some of their innovations eventually paved the way for what would come later. Instead of tinfoil placed over a cast iron cylinder, the graphophone made use of wax-covered cardboard cylinders. These were not only cheaper to produce, but also capable of playing back recordings in greater detail. Bell's development team also pioneered clockwork playback and, later, the use of electric motors to rotate the wax cylinder.

In the United States, a major battle between rival systems began. The American Graphophone Company was formed to market Volta Laboratory's device – and later the wax cylinder recordings of music to play on them – while Edison tweaked his phonograph to play solid wax cylinders.

Enter the gramophone

In the end, it would be neither of these devices that would go on to become the playback

→ Emile Berliner's decision to use flat, round discs instead of cylinders on his gramophone paved the way for the record industry as we know it today

device of choice for music fans. Instead, the dominant 'record player' design would be the gramophone, a machine patented by German-American inventor Emile Berliner in 1887.

Berliner had decided that Cros's method of etching recordings onto a flat rotating disc, rather than a horizontally mounted cylinder, was the way forward. His earliest patented device utilised a zinc disc coated in a thin layer of beeswax. In 1890 Berliner collaborated with a German toy manufacturer to create five-inch-sized rubber discs, before pioneering seven-inch rubber 'records' in 1894.

It took time for Berliner's gramophone to take off, but his desire to offer a range of mass-manufactured recorded discs, or 'records', would eventually win the day. A big leap forward came in 1895, when his American Gramophone Company perfected the manufacture of shellac discs; these would remain the dominant format for recorded music until the 1930s.

Of course, there were still issues with Berliner's early gramophones. For starters, you could only fit around two minutes of music on one of his shellac discs, and there was no standardised playback speed. The gramophone was capable of playing back music at a louder volume – partly due to the superior quality of his shellac discs, but also the oversized playback 'horn' incorporated into player designs – but it was far from perfect. By the early 20th century, though, his device was beginning to win the battle with Edison's cylinder-based 'Perfect Phonograph'.

The birth of the record industry

As the popularity of gramophones and phonographs soared, so did the need for manufactured 'records' and wax cylinders. The first to market was the Columbia Phonograph Company, the forerunner of Columbia Records. They began manufacturing cylinders in 1897, producing their first disc records under licence in 1901.

Columbia was in direct competition with the Victor Talking Machine Company, another player and disc manufacturer who later introduced the famous His Master's Voice label, and its now familiar image of a dog listening to a gramophone. Victor manufactured discs of

↑ Victor Talking Machine Co. was a pioneer in early record players, launching the Victor for $15 in 1902 (Royalbroil)

various sizes, most notably seven inches, ten inches and twelve inches.

Columbia continued to come up with pioneering new developments. First, in 1903, they began experimenting with black wax discs, and by 1908 they'd perfected a method of manufacturing double-sided shellac discs. These sold for 65 cents each and mostly featured recordings of opera singers and classical music performances.

The age of the record player

The development of electrical recording techniques in the mid-1920s, coupled with an agreed standard playback speed of 78 revolutions per minute, helped drive a boom in sales of gramophones and records. RCA Victor pioneered 'long-playing' 33rpm discs as early as 1931, though the lack of suitable playback equipment meant that it was a commercial flop.

The rise of radio in the early part of the 20th century was a worry for the manufacturers of records and the machines to play them on. Although their systems and discs were growing in popularity, neither were genuine mass-market products. Uptake amongst the urban middle

↑ Victor Talking Machine Co. was a pioneer in early record players, launching the Victor for $15 in 1902 (Royalbroil)

class was healthy, but those lower down the economic scale simply couldn't afford to purchase a gramophone.

Following the end of the Second World War, record labels and hardware manufacturers redoubled their efforts in a bid to find a breakthrough. Almost all record players now came with three standardised speed settings: 33rpm for 'long playing' records, 45rpm for seven-inch singles, and 78rpm for vintage ten-inch releases.

By 1955, Philco was ready to introduce its range of 'transistor phonographs': portable battery-powered record players that boasted a built-in amplifier and speakers. They cost as little as $59.95 in the United States, a price within the budget of most working families. Teenagers caught up in the rock 'n' roll revolution could even save up and buy one of their own.

Top of the pops

The boom in sales of transistor phonographs coincided with the growth of pop music on both sides of the Atlantic, as well as audiophile developments such as 'high-fidelity sound' and, of course, stereo recording and playback. Serious music fans began investing not in Dansette- or Philco-style record players, but rather 'turntables' – record decks that would be connected to a separate amplifier and set of speakers. This combination produced much better sound. Plus, if you had the money, you could invest in groundbreaking but ultimately doomed developments such as 'quadraphonic' four-channel sound (an invention heavily marketed in the 1970s).

By the early 1980s, almost every home boasted a 'home hi-fi' system made up of separates – turntable, radio, amplifier and cassette deck in most cases – or a cheap, all-in-one unit available for a fraction of the price. As the decade wore on, though, the rise of digital technology and the 'compact disc' system resulted in sales of turntables and records plummeting. Of course, the format was kept alive by enthusiasts, their desires satisfied by the development of high-quality equipment aimed at connoisseurs.

Today, sales of turntables and vinyl records are higher than they've been since the tail end of the 1980s. What many thought was a 'dead system' is once again popular, with listeners of all ages investing in analogue equipment in order to revel in the warm, rich sound of pressed vinyl discs. The new vinyl era has begun.

↓ The Dansette range of record players was hugely popular in the UK, with over a million units sold in the 1950s and '60s

Dansette

THE ART OF NOISE

Weird and wonderful turntable designs through the ages

Since the dawn of the phonograph in the late 19th century, many manufacturers have developed innovative or artistic turntable designs. Here are four of our favourites:

↓ ELP Laser Turntable

This costly unit looks like an oversized CD player, with the vinyl disc sitting in an oversized plastic tray. Innovatively, it reads the grooves of a record using a precision-guided laser, rather than a trusty stylus, therefore protecting the vinyl from wear and tear. It probably won't make that scruffy 7in single you found in a charity shop sound any better, mind.

(Pdproject – Own Work)

↑ Da Vinci Audio Gabriel

Undoubtedly one of the most eccentric audiophile turntables ever created, the £61,000 ($79,000) Da Vinci Audio Gabriel looks like something NASA may have designed, rather than a record player. It's a modular system that can be purchased in numerous configurations, including the 'Monument' edition, which boasts four separate tonearms (each can be fitted with a different kind of specialist stylus).

↓ Vestax Controller 1

Before going out of business in 2014, Japanese manufacturer Vestax was responsible for a string of innovative turntables. Perhaps the most notable was the Controller 1, a turntable marketed as the first 'DJ musical instrument'. Using the various buttons placed around the outside, you could manipulate the sound coming out of the deck and even 'tune' the record playing, in the way you would a guitar or piano.

← Transrotor Artus FMD

Standing at 1.2m tall and weighing in at 220kg, the Transrotor Artus is something of a beast. It boasts all manner of high-tech, innovative features designed to provide perfect playback, which seems rather fitting given that it looks like some kind of futuristic scientific apparatus.

The beginner's guide to turntables

How does a piece of vinyl capture and transmit the magic of sound? Discover the science behind records and record players, plus other essential information.

It would be fair to say that the science behind how a record player works has not changed in the best part of a century. Sure, there have been notable technological breakthroughs – not least the electrification of the system – but the basic method of 'reading' the grooves of a record and turning them into sound has remained the same.

In order to understand the science, we thought you might appreciate a short guided tour of an average turntable. By explaining what each of the key parts does – and in many cases, how they work – we hope to provide you with a rock-solid understanding of the process. It's actually quite simple – it was developed in the 19th century, after all – though it can seem utterly baffling to beginners.

⇩ Turntable technology may have improved a lot in the last 100 years, but the 'needle in a groove' method pioneered by Emile Berliner remains

What's on a record?

While the answer to this question is obviously 'sound', it's a little more complex than that. If you studied the surface of a record with the aid of a microscope, the first thing you'd notice is that the distinctive grooves we all know and love actually rise and fall like hills and valleys.

Sound waves rise and fall like this when they're represented visually. If you've ever used music production software, or seen someone else use it, you'll have seen the distinctive peaks and troughs of sound waves on screen. It's not those sound waves on the surface of a record, but indentations created by sound waves during the manufacturing process.

If this all sounds a little familiar, it's because

→ Zoom in even closer than this and the grooves cut into the surface of the record look like foothills and mountains rising in the distance

→ Here's how a portion of a stereo track is represented in audio editing software; the taller waves represent louder portions of the track

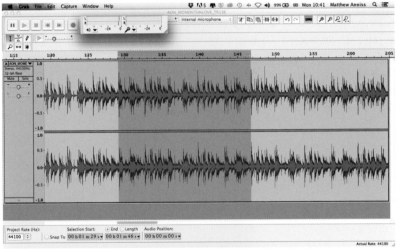

the method of creating vinyl records is still based on the pioneering recording techniques developed by Edouard-Leon Scott de Martinville, Thomas Edison and Emile Berliner. While their machines used needles attached to vibrating membranes to create impressions in blackened paper, tinfoil or wax, vinyl manufacturers now use costly cutting lathes. The principle, though, is the same. You can find more about the vinyl manufacturing process in Chapter 3.

If you remember, it was Edison who first realised that you could 'play' the sounds etched onto paper, tinfoil or wax by reversing the production process. It's the same with records. In order to 'read' the continuous, spiral-style grooves etched onto the surface of a record, the disc needs to rotate. That's where the turntable comes in.

Turning the tables

In the centre of any turntable or record player you'll find a raised metal plate of roughly 12in in diameter. This is known as the platter, and it's this that spins when you play a record.

← To keep the record stable and in place, the platter features a small, centrally placed vertical metal cylinder or tube known as the spindle. The hole at the centre of a record is just a little wider than the diameter of the spindle in order to neatly fit over it

The rotation of the platter is driven by an electric motor. The motor's rotor is connected to the underside of the platter in one of two ways. On 'belt drive' turntables, the motor turns an elastic or rubber belt, which in turn makes the platter spin. 'Direct drive' turntables, on the other hand, fix the motor's rotor directly to the platter.

There are pluses and minuses to both methods of rotation. Audiophiles tend to prefer belt drive decks as the rubber or elastic loop dampens the vibrations of the motor, therefore reducing potential sound interference. DJs, on the other hand, much prefer direct drive turntables, which offer greater control of playback speed, almost instant stopping and starting, and higher torque. You can easily stop and pull back the platter of a direct drive turntable by hand; if you try this on a belt drive deck you may damage the belt.

On direct drive turntables, and some DJ-friendly belt drive models, it is possible to subtly increase or decrease the speed at which the platter spins. The speed of the platter's rotation is measured in revolutions per minute (RPM). All turntables boast at least two standard 'rpm' settings: 33 (and a third) and 45. Some may also have a third setting, 78rpm. Today, very few 78rpm records are

manufactured, though it was the dominant format for the first half of the 20th century.

Generally speaking, 33rpm records tend to be long-playing ones. By cutting records at '33', you can fit up to 25 minutes on one side of a 12in disc. At 45rpm, you can fit around half of that. We'll go into more detail about this, and the difference it can make to sound quality, in Chapter 3.

Super-stylin'

The most important part of any record player is the stylus, or 'needle', and the phono cartridge, or 'pickup', that it's connected to. Between them, they turn the vibrations created by the grooves on a record into electrical signals, which can then be sent to an amplifier and speakers.

The stylus pokes out from the underside of the phono cartridge, which is then screwed onto the head shell. This sits at one end of the tonearm, on the other end of which is a counter-balance.

When gently placed on the surface of a rotating record, the stylus 'rides' the grooves. As it tracks the continuous spiral etched onto the surface, the diamond or sapphire tip of the stylus sends vibrations through a thin strip of metal into the cartridge above.

This is where things get exciting. At the cartridge end of the stylus, encased within plastic housing, you'll find a miniscule magnet surrounded by two tiny coils of wire. The vibration of the stylus moves the magnet, which in turn induces an electric current via the coils.

← This weight can be adjusted to suit the weight of the needle and cartridge. The idea is to keep the cartridge and needle as stable as possible during playback

In other words, there's a tiny electromagnetic generator inside each and every phono cartridge.

This is known as the 'moving magnet' (MM) system. There are other styles of cartridge, but it's the MM technology that you'll find inside most. Some cartridges use a 'moving coil' method (the magnet is fixed and the coils move), while others use a 'moving micro cross' (MMC) technique. In this system, the magnet and coils remain stationary while a tiny 'micro cross' vibrates along with the stylus. You'll find more information on the pluses and minuses of each of these cartridge designs, and the styli that work with them, later in the chapter.

From cartridge to speakers

Regardless of the exact type of cartridge your turntable uses, the creation of electrical current is a constant feature. It's this current that is sent down the tonearm and on to the audio outputs at the back of the turntable (or, if you have an old-style portable record player, to the built-in amp and speakers).

Once the electrical current has whizzed down the attached RCA phono cables, it surges into an amplifier in order to be sent to the speakers. It's at this point where you can alter the dynamics of the sound – more bass, less treble and so on – and increase the volume.

The vibrations of the membranes inside the speakers turn into sound waves as soon as they hit the air. We hear these waves as music, speech or whatever else was recorded and pressed onto the record. The fact that these sound waves are accurate to the recording created by the musicians and producers behind the record is arguably the most astonishing aspect of the whole process. This is archaic technology, after all, but somehow the music we hear coming out of the speakers is warm and rich. That, ladies and gentlemen, is the magic of vinyl.

↓ When you turn up the volume on your amp, what you're really doing is increasing the electrical current so that it vibrates the membranes inside the speakers (known as the cones) with more ferocity

The anatomy of a turntable

This is what a DJ-friendly Vestax PDX-2000 turntable – on sale throughout the 2000s but now discontinued following the company's closure – looks like from the inside. It's a direct drive turntable, which is why you can't see a belt. The model boasts many more features than your average DJ 'deck', which partly accounts for the additional electronic circuitry. You'll find explanations of some of the key features in the annotations below.

① Tonearm base
The metal section is the underside of the tonearm, featuring the simple mechanics that allow it to move and track the grooves of a record during playback. The protruding wires are those that carry electrical signals from the stylus, via the head shell and tonearm.

⑤ Pitch control circuit and ultra-pitch/ start/brake circuit
The circuit board closest to the camera relates to some of the PDX-2000's unique features: ultra-pitch, which allows users to slow down or speed up playback to extremes, platter reverse and start/brake speed adjustment. The circuit board behind it relates to the turntable's pitch control fader. When users make use of any of the mentioned controls, instructions are sent to the direct drive motor via the connecting grey wires and the motor control circuit board.

↑→ With the platter removed, the PDX-2000 is still recognisably a DJ-friendly turntable. Note the protruding motor shaft (right), topped by the spindle and flanked by flat 'wings'; it's onto these that the platter would normally be screwed

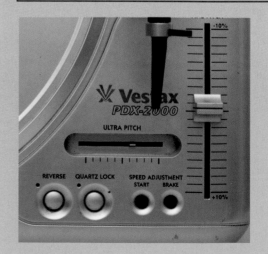

② Motor control circuit board
The heart of the turntable's control mechanism, this circuit board regulates the speed of the turntable's direct drive motor. Information is fed in from other control circuits related to turntable features (pitch control, start, brake and so on), and then onto the motor.

③ Direct drive motor
Hidden inside an industrial-strength casing, the motor rotates the platter and subsequently makes your records spin.

④ Transformer
This takes the mains power and converts it to the 'control voltage' (12v) used to power the turntable's various functions (and, in particular, the motor).

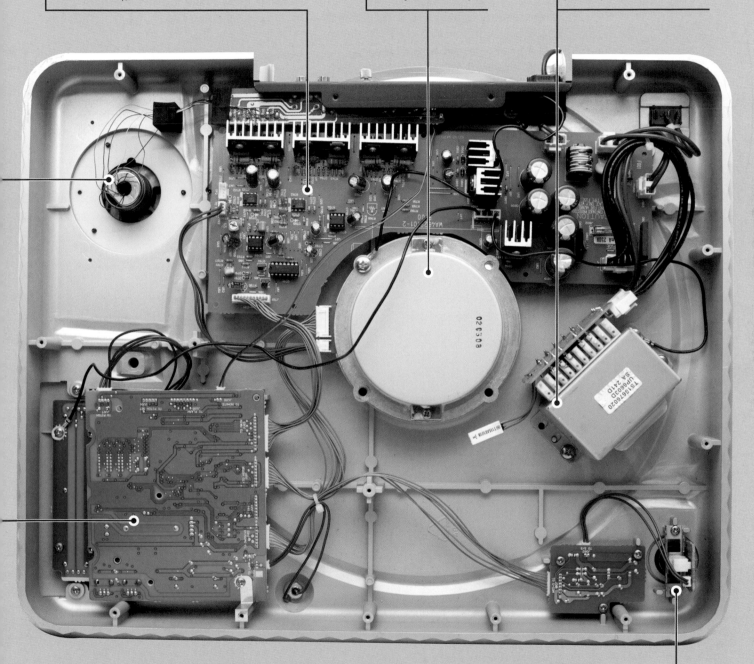

⑥ Stop/start button mechanism
The small circuit board to the left of this conceals the underside of the '33' and '45' RPM selector buttons. When the user presses any of these buttons, these instructions are routed to the motor via the large printed circuit board that also handles the 'ultra-pitch' feature, and the motor control circuit.

How to choose a turntable or record player

Want to buy a 'deck' but confused by the sheer number of options? If so you've come to the right place. We take a look at the types of turntable on offer and which best suits your needs.

Buying something to play your records on can be a surprisingly complicated business. The much discussed 'vinyl revival' has been a boon for manufacturers of turntables and record players, who have flooded the market with a dizzying array of models. These range from simple budget models that cost well under £100 ($130), to all-singing, all-dancing decks that will set you back tens of thousands of pounds.

The best place to start is by working out your budget. Generally speaking, the more money you have to play with, the better. However,

⬇ Vintage-style record players with built-in amplification have become hugely popular in recent years (crosleyradio.com)

unless you're a serious audiophile, there's little point breaking the bank when you can find a top-notch turntable for £500 ($740) or under.

It goes without saying that more expensive turntables tend to boast higher sound quality (though there are improvements you can make by buying better-insulated phono leads, cartridges and styli) and better components. The build quality is usually higher, too, making these turntables more durable than cheap plastic budget decks. These are generalisations of course: specialist magazines such as *What Hi-Fi?* will be able to fill in the gaps in your understanding.

Superstar DJs take control

The next thing to decide on is the type of 'deck' you'll need. If you're thinking of taking up DJing, you'll need to find a turntable with the right tools for the job. That means opting for one that boasts a pitch control fader, which allows you to subtly alter the speed of the platter's rotation during playback.

DJ turntables come in two distinct varieties. Cheaper options tend to be 'belt drive', like most hi-fi turntables. If you're going to take DJing seriously, though, you should opt for a 'direct drive' model. This offers greater platter torque and more accurate control over playback speed. When you dramatically speed up or slow down playback using the pitch control fader on a belt drive turntable, you may hear a woozy sound as the control mechanism adjusts. Belt drive decks are also much harder to keep in time.

These days, you can pick up a solid direct drive, DJ-friendly turntable for less than £200 ($260). To DJ, you'll need two, plus a DJ

← If you're going to try your hand at DJing with vinyl, your turntable will need one of these: a pitch control fader for speeding up or slowing down playback

mixer. You can find out more about the latter in the next chapter, with DJ technique advice contained in Chapter 5.

Record players versus turntables

The next thing to decide is whether you want a turntable or a record player. The former is a 'deck' that needs to be plugged in to a separate amplifier and speaker, while the latter comes with built-in amplification.

Buying 'separates' is a more costly business, though if you're a music enthusiast you may already have an amplifier, speakers and – depending on your age – a CD player. While the set-up costs are higher, if you don't already own 'separates', you get far more control over sound quality. You can upgrade each element in the 'chain' – phono leads, speaker cables, the amp and speakers themselves – at a later date, should you so wish.

Record players are good for those who have limited space, a limited budget or who want to buy an additional turntable. The majority of all-in-one record players on the market today boast 'vintage' styling to make them look like classic designs of the 1950s or '60s. Many are also portable, meaning that you can set them up anywhere – as long as there's a level surface available, of course.

If you're feeling nostalgic for your youth or simply hanker after

↓ Many portable record players boast a built-in speaker and outputs to connect them to an amplifier. This model, aimed at 'scratch' DJs, has also been fitted with an optional crossfader

something that reeks of the golden age of vinyl, then record players are a good option. Sound quality isn't always top of manufacturers' agendas, though, so do your research before parting with any of your hard-earned cash.

Our final piece of advice is to think about any additional features that may be important to you. For example, do you need a turntable or record player capable of playing vintage 78rpm records? Most people have no need, though if you're thinking of collecting classical recordings, this function is essential. You may also prefer a turntable with USB capability. This will allow you to make 'digital' copies of your records (for personal use, of course – sharing digital files of songs or albums is illegal under copyright law) by recording straight into your home computer.

BRAND NEW SECOND HAND

There's nothing to say that you have to buy brand-new equipment. In fact, there's a thriving trade for second-hand turntables and record players. Do a quick search online and you'll find countless specialist hi-fi retailers who sell second-hand 'decks' from the 1960s, '70s and '80s that have been lovingly restored.

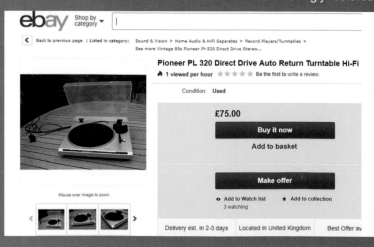

They're usually not cheap, but you're paying for a working antique that will only increase in value if you look after it properly.

Online marketplaces such as eBay and Gumtree are another good place to look for second-hand turntables. If you're after DJ turntables, and Technics 1210s in particular, they're usually the place to start your search. A well-loved pair of 1210s should set you back between £700–800 (around $1,000).

Remember to be careful when buying second-hand turntables or record players, whether online or via 'vintage' shops. A deck may look good from the outside, but it could have numerous playback issues. Where possible, ask for a demonstration. If you encounter minor problems, these may be 'fixable'. There are plenty of trained service engineers out there; if there's a hi-fi shop near you, ask the staff if they know anyone locally who could help.

The world's most expensive turntables

If you're feeling especially flush, these notably pricey models could be for you. We asked the experts at *What Hi-Fi?* to tell us about the ten most desirable decks ever built.

At *What Hi-Fi?* we've seen plenty of different turntables pass through our test rooms over the years, from brilliant budget decks that deliver excellent performance per pound value, to high-end players that have us eagerly revisiting our record collection. But there's still a world of super-high-end turntables that we tend not to get our hands on too often, preferring as we do to feature products that the majority of us are more likely to buy.

The costliest turntable we've ever reviewed is a snip at £30,000, certainly in comparison to some of the decks featured in the list below. Many of these could be considered vanity projects, but there's no denying some of the engineering feats involved. Perhaps the technology will eventually trickle down to more affordable offerings in years to come? We live in hope.

Whether the stuff of dreams or shining examples of audiophile excess, these are our picks of the most expensive turntables ever made. Think of them as the turntable equivalent of supercars…

TOP TEN SUPER-HIGH-END TURNTABLES

TechDAS Air Force One

Price: £75,000 ($97,500)

Air by name, air by nature. How many decks do you know with an air bearing to support the platter, or achieve isolation from its support through air suspension? But it doesn't stop there. Those with warped discs – that's us too – can rejoice in the Techdas's ability to suck a record flat onto its platter, giving the cartridge an easier ride.

Clearaudio Statement v2

Price: £92,500 ($120,000)

The Statement v2 is made from bulletproof wood sandwiched between aluminium plates and can accommodate up to four tonearms, including the £18,500 Statement TT1 v2 tangential tonearm (should you have some cash left over). Unlike the TechDAS there's no air main bearing, with Clearaudio choosing to float the platter with magnetism instead. More realistic Clearaudio turntables are also available.

J.C. Verdier La Platine Magnum

Price: £95,000 ($123,500)

The La Platine is huge, has a 50cm platter (that's a 12in record in the picture) and weighs a colossal 400kg, thanks to a base made of granite. And say what you like about the design, it certainly looks better than the company's website.

Rossner and Sohn MOTT

Price: Up to £105,000 ($137,000)

MOTT stands for Mother of TurnTable and this is one serious mother, with an overall weight of 325kg. There are various specifications available for this German turntable, but the top-end model comes with automatic pneumatic adjustment and an air bearing. You'll have to wait six months for one to be made to order, mind.

OneDof One Degree

Price: £105,000 ($137,000)

The One Degree was designed by NASA space engineer Aleks Bakman and claims to eliminate all resonance thanks to 'liquid suspension'. Naturally it uses 'aerospace grade metals', too. It features 24-carat gold plating and weighs a rather more manageable 23kg.

Basis Audio Work of Art

Price: £105,000 ($137,000)

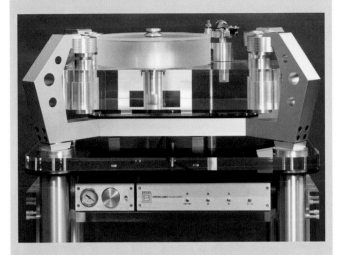

Billed as a 'tribute to the science and art of vinyl music reproduction', this Basis Audio turntable uses a vacuum system to hold the record down on the platter and even claims to be able to restore warped records to 'exact flatness'. There's a non-vacuum version, too, but in for a penny in for a pound, we reckon....

Transrotor Artus

Price: £105,000 ($137,000)

Transrotor hopes your £105,000 will be well spent on the Artus, thanks to the deck's ability to deliver a completely level playing platform using 'cardanic suspension' – a gimbal design ensures it pivots around a single axis. Made from solid aluminium and acrylic, it also features a contactless magnetic field drive and a balanced tonearm (you'd hope so, too). And it weighs a quarter of a tonne.

Audio Consulting R-evolution Meteor

Price: £130,000 ($169,000)

This battery-powered turntable is apparently made from 'one entire tree'. And not just any tree, either, but one that's been dried for at least 20 years. Craftsmen then spend two weeks getting the surface 'just right' by hand. It uses a two-chassis construction designed 'to avoid any standing waves' and can support two tonearms. You can even have the platter in Ferrari red, which is arguably fitting given the price.

Goldmund Reference II

Price: £165,000 ($214,500)

The Reference II was limited to just 25 units, has a platter that weighs 20kg, and some 15kg of brass shielding for the motor. There's no end to the fantastical-sounding features – 'liquid nitrogen-rectified belt' being our favourite – but sadly the £165,000 doesn't go quite as far as you might hope; you'll still need to shell out for a tonearm and cartridge....

AV Designhaus Derenville VPM 2010-1

Price: £460,000 ($600,000)

We think the Derenville VPM 2010-1 might just be the most expensive turntable ever made. You'd expect a great deal of technology in something costing the best part of half a million pounds, and you'd be right.

The VPM 2010-1 has two frequency-controlled motors on the belt, a solid 60kg chassis (made from a special material called Corian, fact fans) standing on four air-suspension feet, laser toe angle measurement and an integrated digital scale. There's an HD camera and screen for checking everything is running smoothly, too, plus a touchscreen remote control.

...AND FOR THOSE ON TIGHTER BUDGETS

You don't have to spend hundreds of thousands of pounds to own a desirable deck, or even one manufactured in limited quantities (which, after all, is part of the appeal of insanely pricey turntables).

In the summer of 2017, Pro-Ject announced the release of two limited-edition turntables celebrating the 50th anniversary of the Beatles' iconic album, *Sgt Pepper's Lonely Hearts Club Band*. While neither come into the budget category, they're certainly affordable.

You could plump for the Essential III: Sgt Pepper's Drum (£430/$560), whose faceplate, platter and slipmat pay tribute to a key part of the album's famous artwork. If you've got a little more money to play with, try the walnut-finished 2Xperience SB. This incorporates some of the same design elements in a refined and tasteful manner and will set you back around £1,200 ($1,500).

Put the needle on the record

Choosing the right cartridge and stylus for your turntable can be as challenging as selecting the records themselves. Here we describe the different types and what they offer.

It would be fair to say that the vast majority of vinyl-owning music fanatics don't know very much about 'pickup' cartridges and styli. Then again, it is a confusing topic, with a myriad of options only making the buying process even trickier.

Audiophiles will gladly tell you that spending a bit of extra money to get a good cartridge and stylus is an excellent investment. We tend to agree. After all, it's the stylus that makes contact with the record and tracks the groove, so even small upgrades can make a massive difference to sound quality. The cartridge is vitally important, too, because it transforms the vibrations of the stylus (and attached cantilever) into electrical signals.

The first thing to know is that when you buy a new cartridge, it invariably comes with the cantilever and stylus tip attached. These latter two elements can usually be removed and replaced at a later date, but we'll come on to that later.

Mounts and moving parts

Before diving headfirst into the world of cartridges, take a moment to study the end of your turntable's tonearm. This will help you ascertain what sort of cartridge 'mount' it has. There are two types: P-mount, where the cartridge slots into the end of the tonearm and is fixed in with a single screw, and 'half-inch mount'. The latter style is generally more

➜ A 'half-inch mount' cartridge attached to the head shell of a Technics SL-1200 turntable

popular, with P-mount cartridges usually found only on budget turntables.

Turntables designed to take half-inch mount cartridges boast a plastic 'head shell' at the end of the tonearm. In this design, the cartridge is fixed to the underside of the head shell using two tiny non-magnetic screws. It's a fiddly process, especially when it comes to connecting the head shell's four tiny wires to the connectors on the back of the cartridge casing. It's not complicated, though, and can easily be done with the right tools (small screwdrivers and similarly precise pliers or tweezers).

There are two main types of cartridge, as we explained earlier in the chapter. 'Moving magnet' (MM) cartridges are the most popular, though serious listeners swear by 'moving coil' (MC) ones. This is because they're lighter and

➜ 'All-in-one' cartridges with internal wiring, which don't need to be attached to a head shell, are available for DJ-friendly turntables

pick up higher frequencies better, therefore producing a better sound. However, they are much more expensive and don't always work with all amplifiers and phono pre-amps.

As you may have noticed while browsing online stores, cartridges vary massively in price. You can get budget models for less than £20 ($25), with prices rising to as much as £12,000 ($15,000). As a general rule, a solid decent-sounding moving magnet cartridge will cost you between £60 and £150 ($75-$190) with the stylus attached.

Stylus tips in focus

So, what do you need to know about the humble stylus? For starters, the tiny tip, which is the bit that touches the record, is almost always made of diamond. Interestingly, there are a number of different shapes to choose from.

The other thing to know about the humble stylus is that it wears down over time. Once the tip becomes blunt, it will start damaging your precious records. Depending on the particular tip, you can get between 250 and 600 hours of playback before it needs replacing (sometimes even more, depending on how well you look after your records).

The first sign of a stylus being on the way out is a noticeable reduction in sound quality. Once serious distortion starts creeping in, you know you have to change your 'needle' sooner rather than later. The good news is that you can buy replacement styli (in their own clip-in-casing) for all but the cheapest cartridges. Our advice is to check your stylus regularly for signs of wear with a magnifying glass. Those that are coming towards the end of their lifespan will look 'blunt' in comparison to fresh needles.

STYLUS TIPS

(AudioTechnica)

Spherical
Most often found these days on budget cartridges, these boast a round tip (as the name suggests).

Bi-radial
More commonly known as 'elliptical', the bi-radial stylus has an oval-shaped tip. It's known for tracking the grooves of a record better than more traditional spherical tips, resulting in superior sound reproduction.

Microridge
Microridge styli are slightly strangely shaped in comparison to their more commonly seen siblings. They take longer to wear out and guarantee great sound throughout their lifetime, but are extremely expensive. The cheapest 'MR' options start at several hundred pounds (or dollars), with the most expensive costing thousands.

Setting up your turntable

An in-depth guide to making sure your turntable is ready to deliver perfect playback, courtesy of the audiophiles at *What Hi-Fi?*

Turntables are arguably the most temperamental of hi-fi components. Inconsiderate positioning, poor adjustment and inadequate support are all things that can upset even the best decks. Get everything right, though, and they can shine in a way that will make you wonder why we ever bothered with digital music formats.

Where vinyl differs from CD or digital music files is the work you have to do to achieve the best possible sound. Unlike the digital alternatives, a lack of care in installation of your turntable can cripple the final sound.

Now there are some great 'plug and play' turntables on the market that not only come pre-assembled, but also limit the amount of work you have to do to get a decent sound. These often come with the tonearm and cartridge attached. There will still be a few things you need to adjust, but these aren't too tricky.

As you move up in price, say £500 and above, it becomes more common that a certain amount of assembly is involved. You can get the supplying hi-fi dealer to do this, but if you fancy doing the set-up yourself, it isn't too difficult.

(Richer Sounds)

For those keen to have a go, a decent toolkit is a must. The bare minimum is a good set of small Allen keys, a set of precision screwdrivers and a pair of long-nose pliers, along with an accurate spirit level. With these you can set up most decks, including fitting and adjusting the tonearm and cartridge.

Steady she goes

The first thing to get right is not the turntable, but the support it sits on. The ideal support is perfectly level, low-resonance and positioned as far away from sources of vibration as possible. And that includes your speakers.

Unwanted vibrations can have a huge effect on playback performance. Remember the tiny diamond tip of the turntable's cartridge is trying to trace bumps as small as a micron (1,000th of a millimetre) and you'll get an idea of just how difficult the task is. Any external vibration will degrade the cartridge's ability to track the groove accurately.

These disturbances can be caused by many different sources: the sound coming out of the speakers, footfall transmitted through the floor, and even passing traffic sending vibration energy through the structure of your house. Yes, really.

When you're playing a record, this unwanted energy is still being fed into the structure of your deck, not only making its life more difficult but also imposing itself on the sound of the record. The result? At best, there will be a slight degradation of performance. At worst, awful feedback that spoils everything.

So, what should you be putting your precious turntable on? On a hard concrete floor, a floor-standing support will work fine, though the same support will emphasise footfall on a suspended wooden floor. If you have such a floor construction, we would recommend investing in a dedicated wall shelf. This kind of support totally avoids the footfall issue. Just make sure you use proper heavy-duty mounting screws and fixings, or the consequence could be expensive.

Most decks have some sort of isolation built in. At its simplest this could be something like rubber feet, or it could go all the way to a fully suspended design. The better the isolation, the

↑ Placing your turntable on a sturdy shelf reduces the likelihood of vibrations interfering with the sound *(Richer Sounds)*

↓ Pro-Ject's RPM 1 is one of the more adventurously styled turntables *(Henley Audio)*

less fussy the deck will be about its support, but even the most sophisticated designs will perform better with careful placement and a good support.

Level up

Whatever the surface or support on which you position the turntable, the deck itself should be absolutely level. This is important, as it helps ensure that the stylus tip sits properly in the record groove. To check whether the turntable is level, use a small, light spirit level.

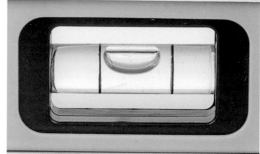

Start with the plinth, which is the main body of the deck on to which the platter and tonearm are fitted. If your support is already level – and it should be – there shouldn't be much to do here. But if, for some reason, you need to make adjustments, many turntables have adjustable feet to help you get things spot on.

Next, check the platter is level. On most decks the platter position is fixed relative to the plinth and should be parallel to start with, unless something's gone seriously wrong in the manufacture. Suspended designs will allow a degree of adjustment.

Usually the levelling can be done in situ, but some decks require a specific jig, which means a trip to the dealer.

Adjusting the tonearm

Most turntables come pre-fitted with a tonearm. If you want to change that, or have bought a more specialist (read: more expensive) deck that comes without an arm, you'll need an appropriate arm board. This is the mounting onto which the tonearm fits. Turntable manufacturers should be able to supply a range of arm-board options, which should suit just about any tonearm out there. As usual, Google is your friend.

Adjustments to the tonearm are normally done at the same time as you set up the cartridge and stylus. We'll talk more about the latter a little later. First, there are a number of adjustments you can make to the tonearm.

Its height has to be set so that the arm is parallel to the record's surface when the cartridge sits in the groove. It's possible to fine-tune performance by altering this so that the arm bearing is a little higher or lower. This alters the angle at which the stylus tip meets the groove – but we'd start with it level.

Setting the tracking weight

Tracking weight is important. If it is set too high the sound becomes dull and ponderous; too low and the presentation will turn thin and the cartridge won't track the groove properly.

If your turntable and tonearm comes with a pre-fitted cartridge (and most non-audiophile ones do these days) then setting the tracking force is relatively simple. If it doesn't, then you'll need to fit the cartridge to the headshell at the front of the tonearm.

Most cartridges are held on with a pair of bolts – these are small and easy to lose, so take care. Some have captive nuts built into the cartridge body, which makes things less fiddly.

← If you're feeling flush and fancy upgrading some of your turntable's components, you could opt for Pro-Ject's 'Signature Tonearm'. Presented in a luxurious, velvet-lined wooden box, it will set you back around €1,900 (£1,700) (Henley Audio)

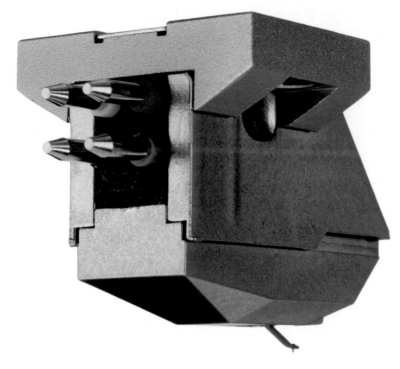

Once mounted, you'll need to connect the thin, fragile arm wires to the cartridge. These are colour-coded but there's not much space, so you'll need small long-nose pliers to help attach them. Be careful when doing this – it doesn't take much to damage the connectors or even break the wires.

Use the force

Setting the tracking force is done by moving the counterweight on the back of the tonearm. At the same time, you should also adjust the sideways force, known as the bias, to compensate for the inward pull of the record groove. The bias is usually set to the same amount as the tracking force.

The cartridge manufacturer will recommend a suitable range of down force, usually between 1.5g and 2.5g, with a specific weight listed as most suitable. That weight would be our starting point but, with production tolerances and the use of different arms, it's sometimes possible to get better sound with a bit of experimentation. It's best to stay within the recommended range, though.

If you overdo the lightness, perhaps in an attempt to reduce record wear, the cartridge will mis-track, damaging the record grooves in the process. Counter-intuitively, if in doubt, go a touch heavier (but not too heavy). The stylus tip will sit in the record groove with more stability, produce less distortion and cause less damage.

Most arm weights come with markings to help, but if you really want to be accurate it makes sense to buy dedicated cartridge scales. While there are expensive – and very accurate – digital options, there are also plastic alternatives that do the job well enough. These only cost a few pounds. Even small errors in alignment increase distortion massively, so take the time to get this right: most deck manufacturers include a suitable gauge.

Take to the stage

Get all these things right and your deck will perform well, though that's not the end of the story. One of the side effects of the move to

digital music has been the loss of a phono stage (also known as a phono preamp) from many amplifier designs.

Even if such a circuit is included within a deck – as it is in quite a few 'plug and play' turntables – it's often an afterthought, with little care taken to maximise sound quality. So what does a phono stage do? It provides extra amplification – the output of a cartridge can be in the order of a thousand times less than a typical CD player – and equalises the tonal balance.

Vinyl isn't physically able to accept large amounts of bass during recording, so the tonal range of the music has to be skewed heavily towards the higher frequencies to make things work. On playback, the phono stage's job is to rebalance this. A good phono stage will let your record player shine. A poor one will have you wondering what the vinyl fuss is about.

If you're planning on turning your hand to DJing and will be looking to buy a mixer, don't worry too much about a phono stage. While the sound quality you would get from a decent phono stage will be similar, a mixer's controls allow you to adjust not only the volume of the music coming out of each turntable, but also certain aspects of the sound, such as the amount of bass, treble or midrange. We'll go into more detail about DJ mixers, amplifiers (including 'integrated' amps, which often include a phono stage) and speakers in Chapter 2.

↑ **A good DJ mixer can provide a more versatile alternative to a phono stage, which allows you to adjust treble, bass and midrange'**

How to digitise your record collection

The vinyl enthusiasts from *What Hi-Fi?* explain how to turn your cherished wax into digital music files, combining the warmth of analogue with the convenience of digital.

We love records. We adore almost everything about them – the look, the feel, the large-scale cover art, the easily readable sleeve notes and the fluid analogue sound. Yet in many situations – whether it's listening to your iPhone, portable music player or computer, or if you've made a move towards streaming – records just won't do.

There is always the option of buying the music again in file form (and some vinyl reissues come with download codes) but if you've already bought it once, the idea of paying for the same music again may not appeal. It's also possible that older recordings may not have made the transition to digital anyway. That's when turning your vinyl records into digital files becomes essential.

↓ Digitising your precious vinyl can be a time-consuming process, but it's well worth the effort

What do you need?

There are numerous hardware configurations, but the basic building blocks are: a turntable (of course), a phono stage, an analogue-to-digital converter with USB output, and a computer with suitable recording software.

It seems complex, but the system can be simplified. There are many turntables on the market with a phono stage, analogue-to-digital converter and USB output built in. Usually referred to as USB turntables, these are a convenient way to get music on vinyl into your computer.

The downside is: most tend to be at the budget end of the market and concentrate merely on getting the job done rather than doing it particularly well. Simply put, your

recordings won't necessarily reflect the quality of sound possible from your records.

Sort some software

Assuming you have a computer, you'll need some recording software. There are many options on the market, some specifically designed for recording vinyl. Channel D's Pure Vinyl comes in at the top end and offers a great deal of flexibility. It features built-in phono equalisation, for example, so you can feed the turntable's output straight into the computer without needing a phono stage in the signal path. It's great, but the downside is a price of around £250 ($325).

A more affordable alternative is VinylStudio. This includes many of the features of Pure Vinyl, including built-in RIAA equalisation, but only costs around £20 ($30). For many people, even this may be a step too far. If that's the case, we recommend Audacity software. It's free and does a good enough job.

Time to record

Before you start recording, make sure your deck is working optimally, the tip of the stylus is free of fluff and the tracking force and bias have been adjusted correctly. These simple things can help produce a better-sounding recording.

In stark contrast to the few seconds that ripping a typical track from CD takes, vinyl can only be recorded in real time. If a song lasts five minutes, that's how long it will take to record. Make sure the player isn't jostled during the recording, and keep the playback volume low to reduce any degradation of sound caused by feedback from the speakers.

Also, make sure your records are spotless and dust-free. Ideally, they would be brand-new and unused straight from the sleeve, but we understand that's not practical in most cases. Remember: any hisses, clicks and pops will be recorded along with the music. You can buy software to remove such sounds afterwards but it's a time-consuming process.

File formats explained

These days, digital storage is affordable, so we'd be tempted to go down the high-resolution route. 24-bit/96kHz is the norm for many studios and seems a good compromise between quality and memory space used. WAV, AIFF or FLAC? It doesn't really matter so much, as long as the kit you normally use is compatible.

CD music or music files usually have metadata built in. In the case of music files this includes album art plus track information. Records don't have this, so the information has to be entered in manually. It's a fairly tedious process but it's essential; without accurate metadata you may struggle to locate the files later.

Your computer won't recognise individual tracks, so you'll have to stop recording when you've finished recording each track. Tracks that flow into each other are an issue too. Mark these for gapless playback or you'll have a few seconds of silence where there shouldn't be.

Once you're done, ensure that you have at least one backup of your digital music library – two is even better. After going to all that effort to record your vinyl, it would be a shame if you had to do it all again.

← If you already have a turntable, the best option is to buy a decent USB phono stage or sound card. Such units pack phono stage, analogue-to-digital converter and USB output in one neat box

↓ Audacity's recording and edit screen may look complex, but it's actually very easy to use

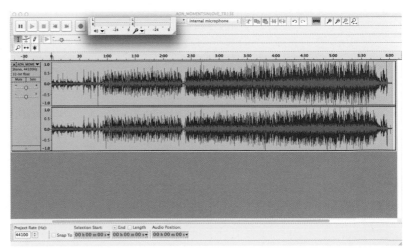

The world's most iconic turntable

How a deck aimed at audiophiles became the DJ's darling and helped to transform the art of live performance in homes, tents and clubs.

In 1979, Japanese electronics giant Matsushita (later to become Panasonic) decided to create two updated versions of its Technics-branded mid-range hi-fi turntable, the SL-1200. Originally unveiled in 1972, the SL-1200 was unusual as it boasted a beltless 'direct drive' system to drive the platter and two rotary knobs to adjust the speed of playback.

The original SL-1200 had not been a roaring success, though it was hardly a dud, either. Serious audiophiles were a little suspicious of

↓ The now-legendary Technics SL-1200 turntable is renowned for its build quality. Most, like this one, have seen a lot of use, but still continue to operate without noticeable issues

the direct drive system and most consumers had no need to speed up or slow down records while they played them.

When it came to updating the SL-1200, Matsushita's designers decided to roll the dice. First, they replaced the usual hi-fi-style automatic start with a quick-response stop-start button. Next, they added a quartz-lock on the motor control circuit to guarantee more consistent playback speed. Finally, they got rid of the rotary knobs and introduced a pitch control fader instead. When it went to market, two versions were released: the silver SL-1200 Mk II and the black SL-1210 Mk II.

Enter the DJs

Audiophiles remained sceptical of the Japanese manufacturer's hi-fi turntable. It didn't sound that great, for starters – in comparison to other similarly priced turntables, at least – and they still weren't bothered about drastically altering the speed of the rotating platter.

Over the years that followed, though, both the 1200 and 1210 began to shift in significant numbers. Matsushita had never put any thought into the DJ market, so were no doubt as surprised as anyone else when pairs of 1200s or 1210s began appearing in clubs.

Yet both models gave DJs exactly what they wanted, accidentally or otherwise. If they wanted to try and create seamless blends of beats to keep people dancing, the deck's pitch adjustment and steady motor allowed them to do just that – as long as they had two units, of course, and some kind of mixing desk.

Some DJs went further, pushing and pulling the platter by hand to create dazzling new noises – what we now call scratching. By the time the rave revolution came at the turn of the 1990s, pairs of Technics SL-1200s or SL-1210s could be found in almost every club throughout the world. It wasn't long before DJing became a desirable pastime amongst those turned on by the emerging dance music culture.

By the time Matsushita's successor, Panasonic, decided to discontinue production in the late 2000s, over three million units had been sold, despite their high build quality meaning that few DJs ever had to buy replacements for faulty models.

Even today, in an age where many DJs have

© audioScope

converted to digital music formats, the SL-1200 Mk II and SL-1210 Mk II remain the standard choice for DJs of all levels of ability. The decks have become so ubiquitous, in fact, that they're arguably the most recognisable turntable design on the planet.

In 2016, Panasonic finally released a new version of the iconic deck, the SL-1200G. Based on the same design, but with a few technical tweaks and improved components, it's a fitting tribute to the original 'Mk II'. As they did back in 1979, the Japanese company insisted it was a turntable for audiophiles and hi-fi enthusiasts, not DJs, with a price point to match. Time will tell whether DJs will be as keen to embrace it.

⬆ **Without the now-familiar pitch control fader, the original Technics SL-1200 looks a little odd, though there is a clear familial similarity** *(Audio Scope)*

⬇ **The audiophile-friendly SL-1200G model is a fitting update of the world's most recognisable turntable**

Chapter Two

Amps, speakers and mixers

Amplification for beginners

If you want to hear your precious vinyl nice and loud, you'll need to get yourself an amplifier. It is, after all, the beating heart of any stereo hi-fi system.

↑ **Modern hi-fi amplifiers combine good performance with suave good looks** (What Hi-Fi?)

↓ **This Tube Box DS2 phono stage has valves to produce a warmer sound, but is expensive at £600**

Once you've bought a turntable (or, if you plan on taking up DJing, two), the next thing to look closely at is amplifiers and speakers – presuming, of course, you don't already own a half-decent stereo system. If you do, it's still worth considering whether you have the right tools for the job; after all, improving these elements is one of the best ways of guaranteeing better-quality sound reproduction.

We'll come on to selecting and setting up speakers later in the chapter. First: a word about amplifiers. As the name suggests, the job of an 'amp' is to amplify the electrical signals being delivered from whatever sound source you plug into it, such as a turntable, CD player or radio tuner.

As you'd expect, there are different ways of doing this. Some high-end, audiophile-friendly amps use valves or tubes, while others use 'solid state logic' (that's transistors to you and me). Some use a mixture of both (a set-up known as 'hybrid'). It's true that amplifiers that boast valves or tubes tend to sound much richer and warmer, but they don't come cheap.

Some hi-fi enthusiasts choose to buy both a 'pre-amplifier' and a 'power amplifier'. The former boasts audio inputs, volume and frequency controls (think 'bass' and 'treble'), a headphone jack and a built-in phono stage. The 'power amplifier', meanwhile, simply boosts the pre-amp signal and sends it on to the speakers.

Power amps come in different classes (A, B and so on), which usually refer to efficiency ratings. Class A power amps are known for sounding fantastic, but they are also rather inefficient, producing rather a lot of power and heat.

Two becomes one

While opting for two different amps gives you more control over the subsequent sound, it's a very expensive option. That's why a really high percentage of listeners opt for an 'integrated amplifier'. This combines both a 'pre-amp' and 'power amp' in one handy box. If you visit a hi-fi store to check out available amps, most on sale will be 'integrated' (unless, of course, you visit some kind of high-end temple of audiophile equipment).

Assuming that you're going to opt for an integrated amplifier, the next stage is to decide on your budget. Just like turntables, amplifiers range massively in price, from solid, budget units that will cost you a few hundred pounds, to models that will set you back thousands.

The difference in price tends to relate to the kind of components used in their manufacture – things like the quality of the circuitry, how well the internal cabling is shielded and what type of metal plating is used on inputs and outputs. Higher quality components don't always guarantee better sound – you can get excellent sounding budget and mid-range models, after all – but as a rule of thumb they do.

Check the 'spec'

Once you've decided on a budget, the next step is research. Have a look at all of the

amplifiers available within your chosen budget and check whether they have the features you're looking for.

First and foremost, your integrated amp needs a built-in phono stage. If you're planning to play digital audio files (or CDs, for that matter) it will need a digital to analogue converter (DAC). Does it also include a 'tone control circuit', which allows you to increase (or decrease) frequencies associated with bass and treble? You should also check the number and type of audio inputs it boasts: you'll need a phono connection for the turntable, of course, but what else do you need to plug in?

The same goes for outputs, too. Those who are interested in getting a home cinema set-up will need to look for a specialist 'A/V' amp with enough speaker outputs to plug in a 5:1 surround sound set-up. Even if you're just interested in good old stereo sound, it's still worth seeing whether there are extra speaker connections on the back.

Some amplifiers boast a second pair of connectors, either to run another pair of speakers in a different room, or to 'bi-wire' one set. We'll explain a little more about 'bi-wiring' in the speaker section, but it's certainly a good option to have. Purchasing an amplifier with multiple speaker connections will make upgrading your system easier down the line.

↓ It's essential to ensure that your selected amplifier has the correct inputs and outputs. If it features a 'phono' input, then it contains an integrated phono stage (Parasound)

How to choose speakers

If you're serious about sound quality, finding the right pair of speakers is essential. We asked the experts at *What Hi-Fi?* to guide you through the process.

↓ Contemporary hi-fi speakers often look sleek and sexy, but it's the way that they sound that really matters *(What Hi-Fi?)*

It's an age-old question: given the vast array of options, how do you choose the right speakers? The all-too-seductive urge in this case would be to buy simply the most expensive award-winner you can afford; after all, if it's the best we think you can buy at that price, doesn't it follow that it's the best for you?

The biggest decision you face is how much you're willing to spend. You'll hugely narrow down your search if you decide upon your budget before seeing what's out there, rather than the other way around. How much you decide to spend also depends on the other components in your hi-fi set-up and whether you may be looking to upgrade those sooner rather than later. There's little point spending huge amounts on speakers if the rest of your system isn't up to scratch, but by spending a little more now, there will be no need to upgrade your speakers later.

Made to measure

The next dreary, yet crucial, task is measuring the dimensions of your room. Firstly, your space may require or restrict you to a certain type of speaker, but it will narrow your search in terms of positioning. Most speakers require a degree of free space to operate in, so if you can only fit them in close to the wall then you need to consider that during your search.

This needn't impact the quality of the product you end up taking home – there are plenty of sonically tremendous speakers that won't mind their backs up close to the wall. Just remember that you're dealing with sound waves that will be affected by whatever they encounter at whatever distance. If a manufacturer suggests you need two metres between its speakers and a wall, it's best not to try your luck.

There are two main styles of speakers: 'floorstanders' and 'standmounters', (sometimes known as 'bookshelf speakers'). Another increasingly popular combination is to opt for a 'subwoofer'/satellite combination pushing the lower frequencies through a sub-cabinet in coalition with a more easily accommodated pair of main speakers.

As a general rule of thumb, bigger speakers tend to be capable of delivering higher volume levels, better dynamics and more bass, though you shouldn't just assume that rings true with every product – it's all relative. Further to that, have a think about the volume at which you're actually going to be playing your music.

Are whopping great floorstanders going to be wasted on you? Are those charming little bookshelf speakers going to breathe sufficient life into your party?

↓ 'Floorstanders' are so-called because they're encased in a freestanding unit and don't need to be put on shelves or speaker stands

→ **Many speakers nowadays also sport four terminals on their rear for you to plug in your cables, which gives you the option of bi-wiring**

↓ **With active speakers, there's a lot going on. However, with no speaker cable in the way you have more control over the sound**

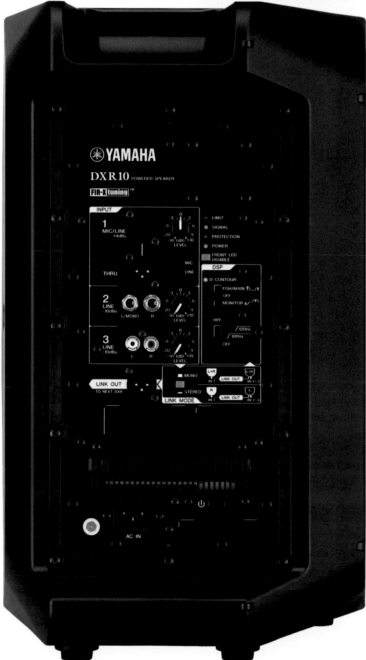

Bi-wired or single-wired?

With a single set of cables all frequencies are propelled toward your speakers together, but if you 'bi-wire' using two sets of cables, your amp can drive upper and middle/low frequency signals separately. The aim is a purer sound with superior precision.

It may be the case that your amplifier won't accommodate bi-wiring, or simply that you aren't interested in doing so. That doesn't mean speakers with four terminals are *verboten* for you – they'll come with conductive links between each pair of binding posts so your music will still reach each driver – but it's worth bearing in mind that a speaker with only two connectors will remove bi-wiring as an option in future.

Passive, active or powered?

You also have the option of passive, active or powered speakers. You'll find most speakers on the market are passive – this means that all the power comes from your amplifier and the speakers direct the signal to their separate drivers via a crossover.

In an active speaker, on the other hand, the signal is separated into frequency bands before being amplified inside the speaker cabinet, which means the speaker requires a separate mains feed.

The main downside of powered speakers isn't so much the cost (they are more expensive – though if you consider the cost of a standalone amp to go with your passive speakers, actives often turn out to be better value), but that if you want to upgrade your system, you're going to have to do so with the whole thing.

We usually find better sound can be accomplished more easily using separate components – a source, amplifier, good cables and a separate pair of speakers – but powered/active speakers, if done well, are an obvious exception.

Another word on power: though less of an issue now compared to the days of valves, if your speakers are demanding to drive, you'll need a suitably muscular amplifier to support them. Don't just look at the headline power figure, see what happens when the impedance drops to four ohms – if the number nearly doubles then your amplifier will be capable of driving more demanding speakers.

How to get the perfect home stereo set-up

Now you're familiar with the ins and outs of choosing an amplifier and speakers, it's time to set up your home stereo. Let the experts at *What Hi-Fi?* be your guide…

So here you are, home again, in the doghouse for spending twice your original budget and facing six months of beans on toast in order to be able to pay for it – but with an exquisite new pair of speakers you already feel more strongly about than you do most of your extended family.

Unfortunately, just like your extended family, they aren't going to do anything for you unless you do something for them first. That means letting the speakers 'run in'. Believe it or not, speaker performance can change with use. All speaker units sound better once they've had a bit of use. Since some speakers take longer than others to bed in and reach their optimum, you'll need to pay close attention to the manufacturer's instructions.

Amazingly, some speakers can take almost 100 hours to come on song, though for most, around 24 hours should suffice. All this really means is you leave them playing, allowing the components to warm up, stretch out and get into their stride. It's unlikely you'd want to do this at any extreme volume anyway, but be careful not to push them too hard straight away. Let them walk before you ask them to run.

(Richer Sounds)

→ **If your speakers have air vents like this at the back, try not to place them flat against a wall** *(What Hi-Fi?)*

with positioning. Really do take your time here, as small differences in position can make big differences to the sonic balance.

Placing your speakers closer to the back wall will give you more bass, while further away will decrease the low end you hear but should offer more convincing stereo imaging. This should be a balance, rather than a compromise, though rear-ported speakers – that is to say those that have an opening or 'reflex port' that allows air to circulate at the back of the cabinet – tend to be more sensitive to proximity to a rear wall.

Do try and avoid placing your speakers in a corner. Despite how convenient it may be spatially, you'll get fat, lumpy bass that'll skew the whole balance. The stereo imaging of the music you'll be playing is also affected by the angle of the speakers and where they're positioned in relation to your chosen listening position.

Get the positioning right

If we accept that you're not really doing anything but plugging your speakers in and waiting during task one, the most time you'll spend getting your system to sound right will be

The mythical stereo triangle

Think of where you'll be sitting to listen – be it on a favourite comfy sofa or in a plush armchair – as the point of a triangle whose sides are of an even length. Opposite where you're sat will

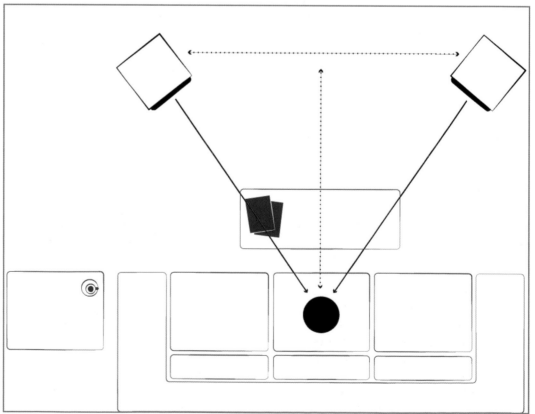

(What Hi-Fi?)

be the 'wide' base of the triangle, with your turntable, amplifier and other separates smack bang in the centre. The speakers should be placed at either end of this 'base', sat on the remaining points of the imaginary triangle.

Measure the distance in a straight line between where you'll sit and your turntable/amplifier combination. It should be directly ahead of you. If that distance is five metres, then your speakers should be set up five metres apart. If you then measure the distance between each speaker and your seated position, it should also be five metres.

This is, of course, a rule of thumb. Most hi-fi speakers sound best toed in towards your most-used listening position, though some manufacturers (such as DALI) design their products to fire straight ahead. Check the manual to see what's suggested for your speakers, including how far apart they should be spaced, the correct inward ('toed-in') angle and the recommended distance from each surrounding wall. Ultimately, it's up to you to adjust and tweak to get the best out of your room.

Stands, spikes and speaker cables

Now, are you sitting comfortably? Well, your speakers would like to as well. You might have bought something advertised as 'bookshelf' but, as with their surrounding environment, the support upon which your speakers sit is of vital importance.

Buy some quality stands. The performance of a standmount, or 'bookshelf' speaker depends hugely on the quality of their supports, so this is another area where you shouldn't compromise. Likewise, if you've opted for floorstanding speakers, make sure you fit the spikes; if you have wooden floors you'll likely have been supplied with coin-shaped pieces to avoid scratching the boards, but, if not, use actual coins. Probably pennies now you've spent all your money.

Perhaps it's an obvious point, but it's as important that your speakers are level and don't rock – a sturdy speaker is a happy speaker. Even if that seems painfully apparent to you, there's a chance you've not considered speaker cables.

When considering what sort of speaker cabling to use in your set-up, there are three key things to consider: resistance, capacitance and inductance. Of these three things, resistance is the most important aspect to look at seriously. If a cable is 'low resistance', then the wire allows more of the electrical current generated by the amplifier through to the speaker coil and cone. Put simply, more power means more sound.

Two things make a difference to the resistance of your cabling: the length of the wire and its cross-sectional area. The latter is the thickness, or gauge, of the wire itself. In simple terms, thicker wires and shorter cable lengths will guarantee less resistance. If you're unsure as to the optimal length of each speaker cable for your amplifier and room, there's plenty of detailed information to be found online.

Most speaker cables are made out of copper, though more expensive silver and gold variants are available. More expensive cables tend to have a higher percentage of actual copper, silver or gold. Whichever metal you opt for, the wire should be properly covered and shielded, usually in flexible plastic casing. Naturally, thicker casing does a better job of protecting the wires inside.

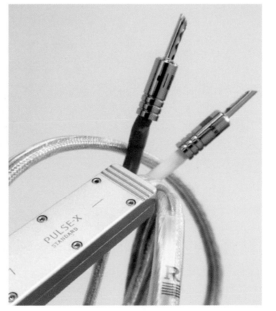

← Some people ignore the significance of good-quality wiring altogether, or try to skimp on the last few quid. Trust us when we say a good speaker cable can be the best value way to upgrade your audio experience *(What Hi-Fi?)*

TOP TEST RECORDS

Before settling in for a night with your now-complete home hi-fi system, it's always worth putting the set-up through its paces. There's no better way to do this than by using good-quality test records – albums that will showcase your turntable, amp and speakers whilst pointing out any flaws that need correcting. He's a selection chosen for us by the *What Hi-Fi?* team:

CHARLES MINGUS – MINGUS AH UM (1959)

Undoubtedly one of the greatest jazz records of all time, let alone just the 'post-bop' period, *Mingus Ah Um* is elegantly played by virtuosos and recorded by people who care. It's full of evocative little details that will simply sparkle, should your set-up be correct.

NEIL YOUNG – TONIGHT'S THE NIGHT (1975)

The late-'90s heavyweight-vinyl reissue of *Tonight's The Night* is one of the most effortlessly revealing records you'll hear. Every greasy finger-squeak, every exhausted bum note in the vocal, every fizzle of the snare beneath the drum-skin reacting to low-frequency sound is delivered with staggering immediacy.

THE CONGOS – HEART OF THE CONGOS (1977)

Dub maestro Lee 'Scratch' Perry's production elevates *Heart of the Congos* from a superior roots reggae album to a peerless and unique recording. During the 'Black Ark Studio' period in which this was recorded, Perry was at his mesmerising best, adding relentless reverb and bizarre noises to every mind-altering stereo mix.

BRIAN ENO – APOLLO: ATMOSPHERE & SOUNDTRACKS (1983)

For a recording during which not much happens – and what does happens occurs at a leisurely and refined pace – this is a much more varied album than some of Eno's earlier ambient work. Drop a copy of this onto a system capable of revealing the 'soft' attacks of Daniel Lanois' superlative steel guitar and prepare for a nice, calming blast-off.

MASSIVE ATTACK – MEZZANINE (1998)

On vinyl, *Mezzanine* is an impeccable recording: one that packs an iron-fisted punch from a widescreen stage. Where scale, dynamics and earth-moving low-end attack is concerned, it's among the most testing albums around. It's a hugely effective album when delivered by the right system.

THE BEATLES – SGT. PEPPER'S LONELY HEARTS CLUB BAND (2017 STEREO REMIX)

We can think of few better ways to test your hi-fi system's capabilities than by whacking on the vinyl version of Giles Martin's 50th anniversary stereo remix of the Beatles' most iconic album. His mixes allow his father George's fantastic production to sparkle like never before. On a good system it sounds mind-blowing.

Sound systems great and small

With enough cash and plenty of imagination you could create a unique sound system, just like these weird and wonderful set-ups from the world of live entertainment.

Big in the game

Unless you plan to try and create Glastonbury's Pyramid Stage in your back garden, it's unlikely you'll ever have to put together a humungous sound system. It's good to know, though, that should you ever need to create a tower of loud speakers to irritate your neighbours, the only requirement is the disposable income to do so.

Pop to any high-quality nightclub – and many festivals, too – and you may well come across a customised speaker system from legendary British manufacturer Funktion-One. Although they do make some astonishingly loud and sizeable 'systems', their specialism is high-quality sound reproduction.

Other sound system builders are less interested in the warmth, depth and crispness of sound. Instead, they build enormous sound systems capable of delivering the heaviest bass and loudest overall noise imaginable.

↓ Sound system specialists Funktion-One are occasionally asked to create mammoth speaker stacks to order. The company set up this colossal wall of F221 bass speakers at a fireworks display in Battersea Park, London (Funktion-One)

↑ **Funktion-One is famous for creating sound systems that get the most out of a venue's natural acoustics. This one, installed at Space in Ibiza, is one of their most famous** *(Funktion-One)*

Many of those who pursue these crazy dreams are naturally obsessed with bass-heavy music. Drum & bass producers Lemon D and Dilinja created the infamously loud and unfeasibly large Valve Sound System in the 1990s, taking it to free parties and festivals in a bid to drown out the music played by rival crews.

Interestingly, the loudest sound system in the world is actually based at the Large European Acoustic Facility (LEAF) in Cologne, Germany. It is capable of producing over 154 decibels, akin to the noise created by a number of jet airliners simultaneously taking off. It's so loud that it has to be stored and used within a nuclear-proof concrete room, isolated from human ears. This unique loudspeaker system is used to test whether spacecraft can withstand extreme noise during launches.

Small but perfectly formed

Others prefer smaller sound systems. In the spring of 2017, Sheffield duo Gerard Jenkins-

↓→ **The World's Smallest Mobile Nightclub, Club 28, began life in Rotherham**

Omar and Stephen Robson (AKA house music production partnership Brandel) made headlines around the world by creating the smallest-ever mobile nightclub.

The micro-club, now officially the World's Smallest Mobile Nightclub according to the team at Guinness World Records™, resides inside a customised garden shed measuring 3ft (0.91m) wide, 5ft (1.52m) deep and 6ft 7in (2m) high. There is just enough room inside for a DJ booth (complete with two turntables, a mixer, a small rack of amplifiers and two speakers), a DJ and a couple of dancers – though we can't imagine that there's enough room to throw some serious shapes. To complete the nightclub feel, the club-in-a-shed also features a mirrorball and some coloured lights.

Since first 'opening' at Rotherham Carnival, where the Guinness World Record was set, 'Club 28' has made appearances at festivals and events all over the UK. The first paying customer was co-creator Gerard Jenkins-Omar's wife, Danielle. His parents and mother-in-law were also amongst the first dancers. 'They absolutely loved it,' he told Billboard.com.

The story of sound system culture

How mobile rigs helped define the music of Jamaica and shape the development of music around the world.

During the 1950s, enterprising young DJs in Kingston, Jamaica, began to put on impromptu parties. Having loaded up a truck with a generator, turntables and huge speakers, they would park up by the side of the road, power up, whack some American rhythm and blues records on the decks and get the party started.

The idea quickly caught on. The first 'sound system' star was Count Machuki (so called because he was renowned for chewing matchsticks), a DJ who would regularly chat over records in thick Jamaican patois. His sound system quickly became more popular at events than bands, cementing the reputation of DJs as the superstars of the Jamaican music scene.

By the time the 1960s rolled around, competition between sound systems was getting fierce. In a bid to best their rivals, DJs and crews would employ the services of specialist speaker builders to create bespoke sound systems. Great sound and heavy bass were the order of the day, a reflection of the key qualities of new Jamaican music styles such as ska, reggae and rocksteady.

The two biggest sound system stars of the period were undoubtedly Clement 'Coxsone' Dodd and Duke Reid. Despite being called DJs, they were mainly MCs, using 'selectors' to play rhythm tracks, over which they would speak or sing.

The intense rivalry inspired both men to become record producers in order to have exclusive tracks – pressed on to vinyl as 'dubplates' – that only they could play. It wasn't long before they were releasing these records for members of the public to buy on their own labels, Studio One and Coxsone (Dodd) and Trojan and Treasure Isle (Reid).

There were times when two or more sound system crews would converge on one spot to do battle for the affections of partygoers. These became known as 'sound clashes' and would feature each of the crews playing records on their system in turn, usually for 15 or 20 minutes at a time. The sound system that got the best response from dancers would be declared the winner.

Global sound clash

When Jamaicans emigrated to the UK and the United States during the 1960s and '70s, they took sound system culture with them. In Britain, regular sound clashes would take place, while similar custom-built sound systems were installed in 'blues' clubs – illicit, unlicensed after-hours venues that sprang up in cities with big Jamaican communities such as Leeds, Birmingham, Bristol and London.

The bass-heavy throb of sound system culture began to be incorporated into British-made music from the 1970s onwards, with bands such as The Clash, The Pop Group, The Specials, Madness and, later, Massive Attack and Soul II Soul all drawing heavily on music made for 'sounds'. Britain's first distinctively homegrown styles of dance music, 'bleep and bass' techno, hardcore and jungle, all borrowed heavily from Jamaican sound system culture.

During Britain's 'second summer of love' in 1989, travelling sound systems – crucial to keep one step ahead of the police, who began to crack down on unlicensed gatherings of people – became popular. Sometimes, several sound

↖←↑ Travelling sound systems became a popular attraction during the rave era, as their owners played a game of cat-and-mouse with the authorities

system crews would come together and throw 'free parties'. If they managed to get to the end of an event without the police confiscating their equipment, the rave was heralded as a success.

Jamaican sound system culture also played a key role in the development of hip hop in the United States, too. DJ Kool Herc, considered by most rap fans to be the godfather of hip hop, was born and raised in Kingston, Jamaica. When he moved to the Bronx, New York, he began putting on street parties accompanied by his own MCs, who would speak rhymes over the music. Herc's ideas caught on and by the end of the 1970s, hip hop had become a recognised style of music.

How to turn your record room into...

Ever fancied recreating a rock festival in your living room, or reclining in a mock-up of the Royal Albert Hall while listening to your favourite symphonies? If so, now's your chance.

At some point, we've all fantasised about having a themed record room, just as some cinema enthusiasts have recreated a vintage 1950s movie theatre in their living rooms. For some of us, the theme may be a particular legendary club we once visited years ago, such as the Hacienda in Manchester; for others, it could be Glastonbury festival or San Francisco's Haight-Ashbury neighbourhood during 1967's 'Summer of Love'.

Here at Haynes we like to offer practical advice, so we've racked our brains and have come up with three record room renovation plans. While not all of our advice is 100% serious, it should at least give you a few ideas on how to spruce up your precious listening space.

The 'rock festival' record room

What you'll need: A large roll of artificial grass to 'turf' over the carpet; A mock stage to put your turntable and speakers on; Metal fencing placed in front and around the mock stage; A homemade banner to hang above it, advertising the name of your festival of choice (or an imaginary one of your choosing); Indoor fireworks timed to go off at key moments during your favourite tracks; A hastily-erected bar serving watered-down, overpriced beer; A dog on a bit of string; Drunken students in band t-shirts; Homemade festival programmes; A guest appearance by The Levellers.

Décor tips: Place life-size cardboard cutouts of your favourite band on the mock stage to

complete the 'Saturday night on the Pyramid Stage' look.

Finishing touches: Get a couple of burly mates to don black clothes and high-vis jackets to play the role of security personnel. Meanwhile, ask a few friends to wander around the room with large flags or banners, obstructing your view of the mock stage. Finally, get that unique 'Glasto' feel by standing around in freezing wet clothes for hours while drunk, wishing you were at home. Oh, wait, you are....

The club in your living room

What you'll need: A couple of power amps; Two sizeable speaker stacks; A powered monitor speaker; A wooden DJ booth to be painted black, kitted out with two decks and a mixer, and placed in the corner of the room; Concrete slabs for the turntables to sit on; Flashing coloured lights; A homemade bar staffed by people who look like they'd rather be anywhere else in the world right now; Moody DJs; Smoke machine and needlessly loud rave siren; Blackout blinds to cover the windows; A local scallywag with his own microphone who claims to be an MC; Tonnes of dance records.

Décor tips: Removing the carpet to reveal bare floorboards will help give your scaled-down club an illicit, warehouse party feel. To complete the look, remove any wallpaper or paint to leave bare brickwork, concrete or breezeblocks. Finally, stick up a few poorly designed dayglo posters advertising DJs with terrible, pun-based names (here are some real ones to get you started: Sell By Dave, Vinyl Richie, Darth Fader and DJ 4Play).

Finishing touches: Gather a group of friends and neighbours to populate the dance floor. Ask a few of them to repeatedly walk up to the DJ and ask him or her to play well-known pop records, inappropriate tracks or simply 'something I can dance to'.

The Royal Albert Hall recreation

What you'll need: Red velvet drapes to hang on the walls; 'Uplighters' strategically placed around the room; A mock stage to place your turntable, amp and speakers on; A small podium to put at the front of the stage; Large wooden panels with intricate wood carvings to place behind the stage; Rows of plush,

comfortable seating; Sofas placed up against the side walls, surrounded by velvet ropes to replicate the luxury 'box seats'; Opera glasses; 4,000 holes (enough to fill the Albert Hall – source from Blackburn, Lancashire, if possible).

Décor tips: The more grandiose, the better. If you have the budget, replacing your regular room lighting with a large chandelier would add a touch of class and put you in the right mood to appreciate the forthcoming festivities.

Final touches: For the first performance of your turntable-powered symphony, invite your richest friends to attend wearing full evening dress. You can act as conductor, raising and lowering the volume of the music during key musical passages. Make sure your guests take regular breaks between records. During that time, they should all stand in another room, drinking wine and moaning about the conductor's performance.

(Colin; Wikimedia Commons)

The story of the DJ mixer

How the demands of a handful of innovative DJs led to the development of a piece of equipment that changed clubbing forever.

By 1971, New York DJ Francis Grasso was ready to unveil an innovative approach to playing records to people. He was not interested in conforming with the accepted approach to DJing, which required selectors to get on the microphone and introduce a series of well-known records. Grasso's idea was revolutionary. Instead of introducing and playing records, he'd mix them together using multiple turntables. Where possible, he would try and create a seamless performance by 'matching' the drumbeats in funk, soul and rock records. In order to do this, he would 'cue up' the record to be mixed in, using headphones. There was just one problem, though: he didn't have the equipment to do this. At the time, nobody did.

Grasso turned to friend, Alex Rosner, asking the audio engineer to build him something that would allow him to showcase his innovations at Haven, one of the NYC clubs where he performed regularly. So, Rosner built a primitive unit hat called 'Rosie'. This pioneering DJ mixer featured inputs for three turntables, sliders (later to become known as 'faders') to alter the volume of each music source, and a cueing function to allow Grasso to listen to music in his headphones before mixing it in.

The birth of the disco mixer

Alex Rosner may have made the world's first DJ mixer, but it would be another audio engineer from New York, Rudy Bozak, who would popularise it. He'd started his career in the 1930s as a loudspeaker designer for high-end audio electronics firm Allen & Bradley, before later striking out on his own to pioneer the development of stereo sound systems.

Bozak began manufacturing sound mixers in the mid-1960s, initially to provide 'sound reinforcement' during orchestral performances. His first commercially available mixer, the CMA-10, featured numerous inputs, knobs or 'rotary dials' to alter volume levels, and high-quality components sourced from his former employers, Allen & Bradley.

When it came to designing his first DJ mixer in 1971, Bozak sought the advice of Alex Rosner and another New York-based audio engineer, Richard Long. The latter went on to build and maintain sound systems at two of the disco era's most famous clubs, Studio 54 and the Paradise Garage. Crucially, Bozak also sought the opinion of a number of leading New York DJs, incorporating their demands into his innovative design.

Unlike Rosner's 'Rosie' design for Francis

↓ **Not only did Francis Grasso invent the 'beat matching' style of DJing, but he also had a hand in designing the world's first custom-built DJ mixer** *(Rutherford Audio)*

Grasso, Bozak decided against using sliders or faders. Instead, he stuck with the 'rotary' dial design of his previous mixers. He added supplementary 'bass', 'treble' and panning controls to allow DJs even more control over the mix of sounds that their dancers would hear. Disco DJs loved Bozak's new stereo mixer, the CMA-10-2DL, as the input volume knobs allowed them to create long, slow blends, or mixes, when segueing between records.

Enter the crossfader

The next step in the evolution of the DJ mixer came in 1977, when a company called GLI released the PMX 7000. Aimed as much at bedroom and mobile DJs as club sound engineers, it boasted Rosner-style vertical sliders rather than Bozak-esque 'rotary' knobs, inputs for three turntables and a microphone, and a three-band 'EQ' to tinker with the bass, treble and mid-range sound frequencies.

Its most innovative feature, though, was a horizontal 'crossfader'. This allowed DJs to quickly segue between records being played on two or more turntables. It was a feature that soon became popular with DJs on New York's growing hip-hop block party scene. Pioneers of hip-hop DJing such as Grandmaster Flash and Grand Wizard Theodore began utilising the GLI's crossfader in their routines, which often involved quick mixing or the creation of unique sounds by manipulating a record during playback (a process that became known as 'scratching').

Since those days, manufacturers of DJ mixers have added all manner of additional features – think on-board samplers, special effects, integration with popular DJ software and 'kill switches' to remove particular frequencies from the master sound – but all still conform to one of two basic designs. 'Fader mixers' loosely based on Rosner and GLI's designs dominate the market, but in recent years the Bozak-style 'rotary mixer' has made a comeback, with some DJs preferring the warm, rich sound provided by the mostly analogue components inside.

(Paul Marshall Photography)

↑ **Rudy Bozak's first commercially available DJ mixers were designed in consultation with leading New York DJs, such as Paradise Garage resident Larry Levan (pictured)**

←↓ **Bozak's rotary design (left) is popular with older DJs and audiophiles, while the horizontal 'crossfader' is an integral part of 95% of DJ mixers (below)**

How to choose a DJ mixer

Sliders or knobs, switches or buttons? Everything you need to know about the DJ and audiophile's weapon of choice.

Buying a DJ set-up is a costly business. It's for this reason that many would-be DJs tend to spend most of their budget on good-quality direct-drive turntables, treating the piece of equipment that ties the two together, the humble DJ mixer, as something of an afterthought. Given that a pair of second-hand Technics SL-1200 or SL-1210 turntables can set you back anything between £600 and £900 ($800–1,200), that's understandable.

Even so, there are good reasons for spending a little more on a DJ mixer. Cheap budget models tend to use lower-quality components, as you'd expect, which naturally has an effect on the resultant sound that flows from the 'master out' to your amplifier. Cheaper mixes tend to be less robust too, meaning you could be stuck with a sizeable repair bill when something goes wrong.

Of course, you can always upgrade your mixer at a later date, once you've mastered the art of DJing and are taking things a little more seriously. When making your choice, balancing cost and build/sound quality should be at the forefront of your mind. Pay a little extra now and you won't have to later.

Before we go any further, it may be useful to understand the two main styles of DJ mixer available on the market. We touched on these in the history lesson that preceded this section, but it's worth going into a little more detail.

The fader mixer

Fader mixers are so called because they use sliders, or faders, as found on studio mixing desks, for many of the key controls. Vertical faders are used to alter the level of sound coming from each turntable, with a horizontal 'crossfader' controlling the mixture of sounds that the audience hears. Fader mixers are the most popular on the market, with prices ranging from less than £100 ($130) to thousands of pounds (or dollars) depending on build quality and specification. Sound quality can vary wildly depending on make and model.

The rotary mixer

Rotary mixers boast large knobs, as you'd find to control the volume on a hi-fi amplifier, rather than sliders or faders. DJs mix by turning these 'rotary' knobs to raise and lower the sound of each turntable. The vast majority of rotary mixers do not use many digital parts, instead favouring analogue circuitry. They have a reputation amongst DJs for providing better sound reproduction and rock-solid build quality. There is, as always, a catch: rotary mixers don't come cheap. Even a small, portable rotary

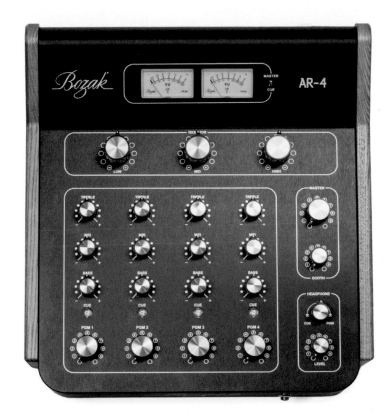

mixer will cost you the best part of £1,000 ($1,300), with market-leading models weighing in at double that.

BONUS FEATURES

Some mixers boast additional features to attract buyers. You'll have to decide whether you need any of those popular additional attractions, as they'll cost extra.

SPECIAL EFFECTS
In-built 'FX' controls allow DJs to add various special effects such as echo, reverb or phasing (trippy stereo panning) to their mixes.

FILTERS
Popular with house DJs, in particular, filters allow you to manually remove certain frequencies by turning a rotary knob.

FX INPUTS/SWITCHES
Use this to add special effects from another source, such as a guitar delay pedal or dedicated FX unit.

USB CONNECTION
Some mixers boast USB inputs in order for you to connect laptops running DJ software. Some mixers even come bundled with DJ software. There are quite a few different applications available, so if you go down this route make sure the mixer supports your choice of software.

MIXER FEATURES EXPLAINED

1 **Channel faders**

Each turntable is plugged into a different channel input on the back of the mixer. In this example, the left turntable would be plugged into channel 1, with the right turntable on channel 2. Some more expensive club mixers boast four or more channel inputs and faders, in order to allow DJs to play music from multiple sources at the same time. While having spare channels to plug in other equipment can be useful, a simple two-channel mixer will be all most DJs ever need.

2 **Channel input switch**

Each channel has 'phono' or 'line' inputs, meaning you can plug in both turntables and digital sources such as CD turntables. These knobs allow you to move between inputs

3 **Crossfader**

The key control slider, this allows the DJ to choose which of the sound sources that the audience hears. When placed centrally, with two or more channel faders pushed up, the audience will hear a mixture of the two sources.

4 **EQ controls**

These allow DJs more control over the sound of each channel. The 'gain' knob lets you raise or lower the master volume of the channel, while the 'high', 'mid' and 'low' knobs offer controls of particular frequencies. By turning the 'low' knob to zero, for example, you can cut out the bass completely.

5 **Monitoring controls**

Sometimes referred to as 'cue' or 'pre-fade listen' controls, DJs use these to listen to sounds before or during mixes. Most have options to listen to sources on their own, the mixer's master output, or a blend of the two.

6 **Output volume controls**

The vast majority of DJ mixers boast two outputs: a 'master out' volume (the sound level being sent to the amplifier) and a 'booth' or 'monitor' volume. This is for connecting a separate monitor speaker or second amplifier and speakers. Some mixers also boast a 'record' out, for connecting portable recorders or a sound card and laptop.

7 **Filter resonance control**

Some mixers have a control knob to change the 'Q' or sharpness of the sound. 'Mild' will give a smooth filter sound, 'Wild' will make it more pronounced, allowing DJs to play with the sounds to build the mood

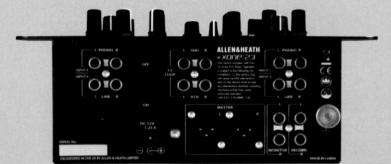

Back panel

The back panel is where all of the leads are plugged in, plus your turntables' grounding cables. Most sound sources will be plugged in using standard RCA phono cables. Output to the amplifier can be RCA phono, quarter inch jack or XLR. The latter is the method most often used to connect mixers to club-style power amplifiers. Mixers that boast 'XLR out' will usually also have an RCA 'phono out' for use with hi-fi amplifiers.

Chapter Three

The sound source

Everything you always wanted to know about vinyl (but were afraid to ask)

Having found its feet in the now familiar flat, circular form, vinyl has changed surprisingly little over the past 100 years. Here we plot its rise, fall and rebirth.

When Emile Berliner's rival to Thomas Edison's phonograph, the gramophone, first went on sale in 1899, few saw a future in the flat, round discs he'd developed to play on them. For starters, in comparison to Edison's wax-covered phonograph cylinders, the sound quality was dreadful. The discs were around five inches in size, could only be played by turning a handle on the gramophone and weren't available to buy in the United States of America.

Berliner persevered. By 1894, he'd developed a larger, more robust gramophone machine capable of playing single-sided discs of seven inches in diameter. These had a recommended playback speed of 70 revolutions per minute, though that was dependent on the machine operator turning the crank at a constant tempo. Sound quality was still an issue, but Berliner moved to address this by working with Eldridge R. Johnson, founder of the Talking Machine Company.

Johnson first helped Berliner to create a motorised gramophone (using a spring motor, rather than an electrical one), before turning his attention to the playback medium. He invested a serious amount of money in improving the quality and durability of gramophone records, as well as the equipment used to manufacture them. By the turn of the 20th century, Johnson's company led the world in manufacturing both gramophone machines and the records to play them on.

← **Berliner's iconic gramophone, complete with amplification horn, has now become a design classic** (*Getty Images*)

Format wars

In the early part of the 20th century, a battle for music reproduction superiority took place. On one side stood Johnson and Berliner, with their new ten-inch and twelve-inch-sized discs capable of playing three and four minutes of music respectively. On the other was Edison, frantically making improvements to his phonograph cylinders – including the replacement of wax with a celluloid covering – in a bid to win over the hearts of listeners.

In the end, it would be 'lateral cut' gramophone records that would win this particular format war. Once initial manufacturing patents had run out in 1919, countless record companies sprung up, each producing discs at the now accepted 78rpm standard. Electrical recording and playback soon followed, though it would take years for these more expensive systems to become popular with the paying public.

Standardisation was beginning to occur in the manufacturing process. Strangely, early gramophone records were made out of all sorts of different substances, including hard rubber, celluloid-covered cardboard (the first 'flexi-discs') and, in the case of Columbia Records' 'Marconi Velvet Tone Record' releases, a fibre-

↑ Thomas Edison's 'Ambersol' phonograph cylinders were an improvement on his original design, but still lost recorded music's first serious format war (Norman Brudderhofer)

core. The latter were a commercial flop, in part due to listeners needing to purchase an expensive, gold-plated stylus to listen to them.

So it was that shellac – a natural plastic scraped off the bark of trees found in India and Thailand – became the base substance of choice for records. Shellac was mixed with minerals (usually slate or limestone), a few cotton fibres (to add strength) and a dash of carbon black to make the record more appealing visually. Until the 1950s, 10in shellac discs remained popular with home listeners, though the format was living on borrowed time.

The first vinyl records began appearing in the early 1930s, though their use was initially restricted to professional applications such as radio shows. While vinyl records boasted noticeably less surface noise, the equipment needed to play them – including higher-quality pick-ups and styli – was beyond the reach of most home listeners.

← Until the late 1940s, almost all records were made of a Shellac-based compound and played at 78rpm (Mediatus)

The microgroove era

Interestingly, it was the Second World War that helped vinyl to become the format of choice in record manufacturing. Due to shellac supplies running low, the United States government opted to use vinyl when manufacturing special 'V Disc' releases – morale-boosting records pressed up and sent to soldiers, sailors and airmen stationed around the world.

There were just over 900 V Disc releases shipped out between 1943 and 1949. These were a mixture of 78rpm and 33rpm records containing an eclectic mix of material, including jazz, classical symphonies, swing hits, radio shows and comedies. The US government paid for stars of the day, such as Bing Crosby, Fats Waller, Duke Ellington and Frank Sinatra, to record special releases.

One famous example, from December 1943, included an introductory message of support from arguably the most famous bandleader of the war years, Glenn Miller. He'd been told he was too old to be drafted into the US Army and go on active service, and saw music-making as doing his bit for the war effort.

During the post-war period, the world's two leading record labels of the time, Columbia and RCA Victor, started championing new vinyl formats – and, of course, the machinery to play them on. On 18 June 1948, Columbia unveiled its new 'microgroove' 33rpm long-playing records, capable of storing up to 52 minutes of music. At the same time, they also started marketing 7in singles pressed at 33rpm.

Their competitors had decided on a different approach. In March 1949, RCA Victor unveiled their great innovation: 45rpm seven-inch singles. These contained a large centre hole to make them compatible with 'auto changer' record players and quickly grew in popularity. Sales were helped not only by the emerging rock 'n' roll boom of the 1950s, but also by increased sales of commercial record players designed to be placed in bars, restaurants and other public places: jukeboxes.

It's no lie to say that jukeboxes had an enormous impact. Particularly popular were pioneering models from the Seaburg

Corporation, who had released the first '45-only' machine in 1950. Their MC100C units became iconic during the rock 'n' roll era, later featuring in the title sequence of TV comedy *Happy Days*.

People from all walks of life could listen to their favourite pop hits, as well as the hottest new releases. Countless record labels sprang up, particularly in the United States, to service the public's seemingly insatiable appetite for 45rpm 'singles', so called because they usually boasted one song per side. As the 1950s progressed, the cost of record players tumbled, allowing more people than ever before to play records at home. The vinyl age had arrived.

Long-playing dreams

It took a series of groundbreaking albums to break the hold that 7in singles had over the buying public. Although they'd been on sale as long as '45s', 'LPs' only began to catch the imagination in the mid to late 1960s. This was primarily an artist-driven development. Record labels had previously treated LPs as a supplement to singles, but groundbreaking sets from the likes of the Beatles and the Beach Boys proved that albums could be so much more than mere collections of songs that could be performed live.

As the 1960s turned into the 1970s, the idea of 'concept albums', where songs or instrumentals were connected by a unifying theme, gained popularity. Sales reflected this shift in emphasis, with sales of 7in singles being dwarfed by those of LPs. This is sometimes referred to as the 'golden age' of the album, when chart-topping sets were capable of selling millions of copies around the world.

↑ Seaburg's classic jukebox designs, such as this one, became a familiar sight in coffee bars and pubs throughout the late 1950s and early '60s
(Joe Mabel)

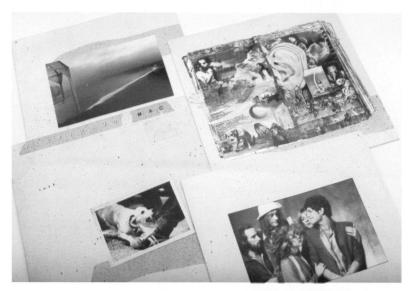

↑ During the 'golden age' of vinyl, it was not uncommon to see bands releasing sprawling double albums in luxurious artwork. Fleetwood Mac's 1979 set *Tusk*, which included multiple inner sleeves, is one such example

INSIDE AND OUT

We've become accustomed to slowly watching the stylus track the groove of a record, gradually moving towards the centre. Not all records play this way, though. Some records, such as Reese's 1991 techno classic 'Inside Out' or 'The Grand Son of Detroit Techno' by Omar-S (2007), are 'reverse cut', meaning that the groove begins near the centre and plays outwards. Interestingly, although the groove direction has been reversed, they still play forwards, unlike the 2011 pressing of Tyree's 'Nuthin Wrong'. Bizarrely, the B-side of that record is not only cut inside-out, but also plays backwards; to hear the correct version, listeners need a turntable that boasts the rare 'reverse' function.

Another freaky and rarely spotted pressing trick is the 'double groove'. These are effectively records with two continuous spirals, rather than one, on the same side. Arguably the most famous example of this is *The Monty Python Matching Tie and Handkerchief*, a typically eccentric and silly set from the British surrealist comedy troupe. Initial pressings featured two different sets of sketches on side B; which you heard was dependent on where you placed the stylus.

As the 1980s rolled around, another relatively new format, the 12in single, began to make its mark. Originally developed for DJs during the disco boom of the late 1970s, 12in singles allowed music-makers the ability to release longer songs and bespoke extended versions. British ambient house pioneers, The Orb, later pushed the 12in single to its logical extreme, releasing a near 40-minute single, 'Blue Room', in 1992. Naturally, the track was split into two parts for the 12in release.

Bust and boom

The advent of compact discs and, later, digital downloads, naturally had an adverse effect on vinyl sales. By the turn of the millennium, most sizeable record labels had stopped pressing up records altogether, with those specialising in niche buyers such as DJs and record collectors, manufacturing releases in far smaller numbers.

All that has changed now, though. Over the last five years there has been a discernible 'vinyl revival', a trend fired by a mixture of older listeners returning to the format and younger buyers who cherish the format's physicality and famous analogue sound. The annual Record Store Day event, which began in 2017, has also played a part in the increase of vinyl sales. In 2017 alone, 89,000 12in singles and 547,000 vinyl albums were sold in 'RSD week' – the highest seven-day figure, outside of Christmas, since 1991.

↑ Vinyl-hungry shoppers queuing to get into a Richer Sounds-hosted Record Store Day event

From the recording studio to the record shop

Have you ever wondered how vinyl records are made? We have, so we decided to get the lowdown from those who make a living out of turning studio recordings into flat, round discs of joy.

↓ **Manufacturing records is a hot and sweaty process that has changed relatively little over the last half a century**

Imagine for a moment that you're in a band that's just finished recording its first album. After months of painstaking work, your producer has completed the final 'mixdown', delivering final mixes of each song ready for production. Your record label has approved them, readied the artwork and decided to commit your work to wax. So what happens next?

Mastering the art

First of all, the album will need to be mastered. This is the process of producing versions of the songs that will go into production and eventually be released. Different music formats each have different demands, so mastering engineers – experienced audio experts who know exactly how to make each song sound its very

best – will need to prepare masters for each. Sometimes, that can mean doing a different set of 'masters' for CD, digital download and, of course, vinyl.

Mastering is a hugely specialist job. Experienced engineers with a good reputation can charge significant sums of money for their time. They need to know exactly how to make songs sparkle, turning unpolished studio recordings and basic mixes into audio gems.

'We try and step in quite early in the process and make sure that the band, producer and record label are all sympathetic to the demands of mastering,' says Shawn Joseph, director and head engineer at Optimum Mastering, a specialist studio and vinyl 'cutting house' in Bristol. 'That means leaving headroom so that we can make fine adjustments to the sound. That helps us get an exciting end product.'

Joseph is one of the most experienced mastering engineers in the UK. Alongside his business partners, he established Optimum in 2004 after years working in other mastering studios.

'I think mastering should be a collaboration between the artist and the engineer,' he says. 'Personally, I want to understand how the artist wants to be represented and what they're trying to achieve. I'll focus on the best aspects of the artist's creation and try and carry those through the whole release. It's my job to turn their work into something really special.'

Optimum is one of only a handful of mastering studios in the UK with the equipment to not only create digital masters tailored to vinyl releases, but also 'cut' the lacquer discs used in record manufacturing. Joseph, then, has both the experience and the tools to ready LPs and singles for release.

'When I'm preparing to commit a track mastered for vinyl to lacquers, there are a few things I need to pay attention to before sending it to the cutting lathe,' he says. 'It's really the high and low frequencies that need the most attention. Bass frequencies need to be in "phase", which means close to mono, as near to the middle of the stereo field as possible. I can check that using something called an elliptical equaliser. If those frequencies aren't in phase on the mixes I receive, then I can sort that out.'

Big and small excursions

The reason mastering engineers worry about high and low frequencies so much during the lacquer-cutting process relates to the way that the cutting lathe (the machine that etches the spiral grooves onto the surface of the special, pre-production discs) makes its mark.

The lathe is a bulky unit, but in effect is like a record player in reverse. Like a turntable, it boasts a platter, on which lacquer discs to be 'cut' sit. It also features an oversized, industrial-style tonearm. Like a regular 'deck', it has a stylus – made out of rock-hard ruby and heated – that etches the spiral grooves into the surface of the lacquer. Joseph describes the lacquer disc as a 'super-flat aluminium disc covered in a thin layer of soft, cellulose nitrate'.

When the head of the lathe digs into the surface of the lacquer's top layer, it not only makes vertical impressions (that's downwards), but also horizontal ones. This means that the spiral being 'cut' into the surface layer looks like a wavy line, with low frequencies resulting in wider 'waves' (or what Joseph refers to as 'excursions'), and higher frequencies being represented by tighter, shorter waves.

↑ **Optimum's Neumann VMS70 cutting lathe features a microscope, through which the cutting engineer can inspect the depth and quality of the lacquer cut**

'With a bass sound, there will be a big excursion when you cut the lacquer, meaning that the head of the lathe will significantly move from side to side,' Joseph says. 'High-end frequencies will be cut in a tighter line with not much left and right movement. We can still cut it, but the stylus will have trouble playing it back. The needle will jump out of the groove and try and find itself, which is what you hear as distortion.'

Specialist 'cutting engineers' such as Joseph have a number of tools at their disposal: limiters for capping sound frequencies, a scaled-down mixing desk and various equalisation controls, to help reduce the likelihood of problems occurring.

'There are different things we can do during the mastering process before we even get to the cut,' he says. 'We can also tweak things just before we make the cut on the lathe. When we send a lot of energy to the lathe and it draws a lot of current, the machine effectively says, "hold on, we need to make sure this is a safe cut".' To be 'safe', a cut lacquer must be playable on a regular turntable without distortion or stylus skipping.

When a cutting engineer such as Shawn Joseph is satisfied that the sound levels and frequencies have been adequately tweaked, he or she will do a number of test cuts using old, scrap lacquers with a bit of free space on them. Depending on the type of record being committed to the lacquers (one disc for side A, once for side B), these test cuts will either be played back on a turntable fitted with a high-end audiophile stylus, or on a bog-standard DJ set-up.

Cutting the lacquers

Once the engineer is happy to proceed, he or she will carefully unpack a fresh 14in lacquer disc and inspect it for potential defects. There are now only two lacquer disc producers in the world, and as each individual 'plate' is made by hand, it's not uncommon to find craters or accidental fingerprints. The scarcity of producers also means high prices, with a box of 25 pairs of lacquers costing around £1,000 ($1,300).

Once the surface of the lacquer has been approved, the engineer will place it onto the platter of the cutting lathe and turn on the suction system that holds the disc tightly in place (the lathe also boasts a second suction device to remove post-cut waste matter, known in American slang as 'hot chip').

The desired speed and record diameter size (12in, 10in or 7in) is then set, so that the head of the lathe knows where to begin and end. Next, the engineer will cut a short silent groove around using the spare two inches around the side of the disc. 'Once we've cut the silent groove I'll look at it through the microscope attached to the lathe to make sure that it's nice and clean, and that the depth and pitch settings are doing what they're meant to,' Joseph says. 'If everything is good with the test cuts and the silent groove, we'll then proceed with the main cut, when we commit the songs destined to be on that side of the record to the surface of the lacquer.'

As the lacquer is being cut, Joseph will keep a close eye on Optimum's vintage Neumann VMS70 cutting lathe, which first went into service in the early 1970s. Manufacture of lathes ceased many years ago, with companies such as Neumann no longer offering spare parts or servicing – something that causes frequent headaches for cutting houses around the world. 'The lathes are getting harder and harder to look after, just at the point when vinyl sales are booming again,' Joseph says. 'We often have

to fly old service engineers in from different parts of the world. Getting spare parts is almost impossible. It's possible to get individual parts specially made, but the costs are astronomical.'

Once both lacquers – one for side A, and one for side B – have been cut, inspected and approved, they're then packaged up to be sent off to the record label's chosen pressing plant. 'We put the two sides opposite each other, with the delicate cut sides facing inwards, separated by a spacer,' Joseph says. 'They're bolted through the box so that they don't move in transit and all of the seals are taped up. We keep the boxed lacquers away from heat and sometimes even keep them in a fridge, just to protect the groove detail, before being picked up by a courier.'

Turning lacquers into records

When the lacquers turn up at the vinyl pressing plant, production begins in earnest. Before any records can be made, hardwearing metal copies, known as 'stampers', have to be created. It's these 'stampers' that will ultimately be used to mould a heated polyvinyl compound into finished records.

'Once the lacquers have been inspected under a microscope and checked against our paperwork, then the production process

← A hard metal negative, known as a stamper, ready to be fitted to a moulding machine or 'record press'

can begin,' says Mirek Hlousek, Head of Vinyl Manufacturing at GZ Media in the Czech Republic, currently the world's single biggest producer of records. 'There are two ways of creating the metal stampers. The traditional method involves lacquers, and the other is called Direct Metal Mastering, or DMM. In the second process, we cover a steel plate with a thin layer of copper and then cut straight into that with a special DMM lathe. There are only 22 of these lathes in the world and we own four of them.'

The key to the creation of metal stampers is a process of 'electroforming', where lacquers or DMM plates are placed in a chemical bath that has an electric current running through it. By the time the lacquers enter the first stage of electroforming, they will already have been rinsed with demineralised water, degreased and coated in a thin layer of silver.

'We put the silver-coated lacquer into the electroforming chemical bath, which contains a solution containing nickel salt and other ingredients,' Hlousek explains. 'The electric current running through the bath helps the nickel attach itself to the silver-coated lacquer. When the process is completed there is a layer of metallic nickel that we can separate from the original lacquer. This is a mirror image of the lacquer and is called the "father".'

This one-off (only one 'father' disc can ever be made from a lacquer as the latter often gets damaged during the electroforming process) will then be put into another chemical bath. This second electroforming procedure is used to create a second, even harder nickel disc called the 'mother'. 'The mother is effectively a playable metal version of the original lacquer,' Hlousek says. 'You can play it on a turntable and hear what the finished record will sound like.'

→ A lacquer disc being 'silvered' ahead of electroforming

← The nickel 'father' after it has been separated from the lacquer disc following electroforming

Stampers and moulding machines

If you're producing records from lacquers, the 'mother' will be put through another electroforming bath to create an 'unformed stamper' – the metalwork fitted to the moulding machine (popularly known as a 'record press'). In the alternative DMM method, the freshly cut steel/copper master disc is put straight into an electroforming bath to create a nickel negative that acts as the unformed stamper.

Whichever method GZ Media uses, the resultant stampers need a little care and attention before they can be fitted to the record presses. 'Each stamper has to be polished so that they become completely smooth,' Hlousek says. 'Then we have to cut the centre holes and trim the stampers to the exact size of the record that you want to manufacture. Then the stampers can be fitted to the moulding machine – one on the bottom of the pressing mechanism, and one facing it at the top of the press. Once you've done that, you can start manufacturing records.'

At GZ Media's plant in the Czech Republic, machine operators are expected to manufacture a single record in between 25 and 35 seconds. 'When the pressing machine is open, with stampers fitted, you put a perfectly dry and heated printed centre label on each side

and what looks like a donut of the polyvinyl compound. This is heated to between 160 and 170°C (320–338°F),' Hlousek explains. 'Then you close the moulding machine, or press, and a record is formed inside.'

During the pressing process, an astonishing 100 tonnes of pressure is exerted on the heated polyvinyl compound. Once the machine is opened again, an almost complete record will be staring back at the operator. They're then required to trim the record to the correct size

↑ GZ Media manufactures its own polyvinyl compound – the raw material that will be heated to an exceedingly high temperature in order to create a malleable mixture that can be turned into finished records. Their formula includes vinyl chloride, vinyl acetate, additives, stabilisers, lubricant and black carbon for colouring

← GZ Media's factory includes both automatic and manual record pressing machines. This is one of their automatic Alpha Toolex presses

→ GZ Media's factory also prints and produces full-colour artwork and packaging

and quickly polish the rough edges off the disc. Once that's done and both sides have been inspected for visual blemishes, the record is put into a box and the operator can then move onto manufacturing the next copy.

'After every five records we put into the box, we add a metal plate to help cool them down,' Hlousek says. 'Once we've finished pressing up a release, the records will be left to cool for eight hours before being sent to be packaged up. That's when they're put into their sleeves and boxed up to be shipped out.'

GZ Media's vinyl manufacturing facility is one of the most historic in the world. It opened in 1951 during the Soviet era and has been pressing records continuously ever since. The plant currently produces around 80,000 records a day.

'In 2017, GZ Media will manufacture more records than we ever did at the peak of production in the late 1980s,' says Michal Sterba, the company's chief executive. 'Of course, the total volume worldwide is still significantly smaller than it was during vinyl's heyday. There used to be big global plants that manufactured hundreds of millions of records a year, but now there are only independent manufacturers like ourselves. For comparison, EMI's plant in Holland used to make around 60 million records a year when it was open, and this year we'll produce around 26 million.'

GZ's giant plant also boasts CD and DVD manufacturing facilities, as well as a printing house and mastering studio. That means that they can offer record labels a one-stop solution. 'We like our customers to come to us and say: "This is what we want from the records and the packaging we'd like you to produce." We like to manufacture the complete product from start to finish.'

Getting to the shops

The final step in the process of getting records from the studio to the stores is distribution. The job of a distributor is very simple: to get record shops to stock their records.

↓ A package of new releases sent by a distributor to the Idle Hands record shop in Bristol, England

They way they do this has changed a fair bit over the years. In the old days, it was not unusual to see distributors driving round the country in vans loaded with boxes of new records, visiting shops to try and interest the owners in buying copies to then sell on to customers.

Today, most distributors add short sound clips of forthcoming releases to their websites. Many also send out weekly emails listing forthcoming releases and back catalogue stock. Distributors will try and build up a relationship with store owners and 'buyers' – shop staff tasked with ordering new stock. Buyers tend to be experienced staff with a good working knowledge of not only what sells, but also which records are likely to be attractive to the type of shoppers who visit their store.

It's not uncommon for certain new releases to 'sell out' at the distributors before release. This means that shops have snapped up every available copy. When this happens, distributors often ask record labels to order a 'repress' – a fresh batch of copies that will be manufactured by the pressing plant that had the original release.

The profit margins on vinyl are relatively slim, especially for small record labels pressing up releases in low quantities. As an example, to manufacture 300 copies of a 12in single with full-colour centre labels (but no printed sleeve) would cost roughly £1,000 ($1,300), inclusive of mastering and lacquer cutting. This means a 'cost per unit' price of £3.30 ($4.20) or thereabouts.

A distributor would then sell this into shops at a 'dealer price' of between £4.50 and £5 ($5.85–6.50) per record – meaning the label could make a profit of £350 to £500 ($450–650) if the release is a sell-out. Of course, that 'profit' doesn't take into account any additional costs of releasing the record, such as paying the artist, sales taxes or employing a PR company to promote the release.

When it comes to doing a repress, costs are naturally lower – you only need to pay for mastering and lacquer cutting once, after all – meaning higher profit margins. Pressing up 300 more records would cost around £700 before tax, meaning an extra £1 of profit per release, assuming that all copies are sold.

WHEN VINYL PRESSINGS GO WRONG

Given that pressing plants manufacture millions of records a year, it's perhaps unsurprising that errors sometimes occur. Occasionally, labels are incorrectly printed, or fixed to the wrong records. These instances are known as 'misprints'. If a record is incorrectly pressed and either sounds unplayable or contains the wrong music, you've got a 'mispress'. Most pressing errors are spotted during the production process, but occasionally some will make it into record stores. On rare occasions these become sought-after collectors' items, but in most cases they're worthless.

To cut down on costly errors such as these, pressing plants tend to manufacture a small number of 'test pressings', which are sent to record labels for approval. If they're happy, then manufacture of the full batch – be it 300 copies or 300,000 – can then proceed.

All records great and small

Vinyl may be round and flat, but it comes in different sizes, colours and speeds. Read on to find out the different formats to make your collection complete.

12in singles

Pioneered during the disco era, 12in singles have long been the vinyl format of choice for DJs. They can be cut at either 33 or 45rpm, with the latter allowing for louder cuts of tracks less than ten minutes in length. During the 1980s, it became fashionable for record labels to release 12in singles featuring extended versions or club remixes of rock and pop hits, as well as dance records. These days, 'twelves' tend to be pressed in limited quantities with DJs and alternative music enthusiasts being the primary consumers.

Long-playing albums

Also 12in in diameter, LPs are cut at 33rpm and can include up to 26 minutes per side. However, cramming in more music means that the record's grooves are cut more closely together. That results in weaker bass frequencies and an overall reduction in sound quality. It's for this reason that albums aimed at DJs often include the same number of tracks stretched across two records, rather than one, allowing for louder cuts of each song.

10in singles

Although now a novelty, ten inches was once the standard size for shellac and vinyl records. The earliest albums were not 'long-playing' 12in records, but rather boxed collections of 10in records. They can naturally fit a little more music on each side than a 7in single, especially when cut at 33rpm. Interestingly, many 'dubplates' (see overleaf) are cut at this size, though 12in 'plates' are becoming increasingly popular.

7in singles

The format that fuelled a sharp rise in sales throughout the 1950s and early '60s, the humble 7in single remains hugely appealing to record collectors. Because they were traditionally cheap to produce, many bands or small record labels opted to produce these rather than albums or 12in singles during the punk era. It's these 7in singles, especially those pressed up in small quantities, which usually set collectors' pulses racing.

Flexi-discs

First put on sale in 1962, plastic 'flexi-discs' were a common sight up until the 1980s. Due to the thin material used in their manufacture, the grooves on flexi-discs aren't particularly deep, resulting in poor sound quality. During the golden age of vinyl, magazines often used to give away flexi-discs containing exclusive tracks or hits of the day. Between 1980 and 1983, there was even a British music magazine called *Flexi-Pop*; naturally, each issue came with a free flexi-disc.

Picture discs

Elektra Records subsidiary Metronome Records was the first to introduce these novelty items in 1970. While they play like standard albums or 12in singles, they feature full-colour artwork across the surface of one or more sides. By and large, picture discs are normally pressed up in relatively small numbers as 'limited edition' releases to tempt hardcore fans and record collectors. These days, it's more common to see coloured vinyl releases rather than full-on picture discs.

Dubplates

Traditionally, dubplates were one-off lacquer 'acetates' produced on cutting lathes for DJ use. The first dubplates were produced in Jamaica for use during 'sound clashes' between rival sound system crews, but they have since become popular with the drum & bass, dubstep, grime, house and techno scenes. Today's dubplates are usually cut straight to blank polyvinyl discs (effectively records with nothing on), using either a traditional cutting lathe or a 'Vinylrecorder' machine, and are said to be as durable as regular records. If you'd like to cut one of your own, a 12in dubplate will set you back around £50 ($65) – a relatively small price for a genuine 'one-off'.

Timecode vinyl

Timecode vinyl is sometimes also referred to as 'control vinyl'. These records are used in conjunction with a laptop, audio interface and DJ software. Their grooves contain no music, but rather electrical signals used by the software to keep track of changes in playback speed and direction. You can find out more about how timecode records and 'digital vinyl systems' work opposite.

The secrets of timecode vinyl

Introducing 'digital vinyl systems', a very 21st-century fusion of vintage analogue technology and modern computer science.

Take a brief look at the surface of a 'timecode' disc, and you'd be forgiven for thinking that it was a regular record. Yet these wonders of hybrid digital and analogue technology contain no music. In fact, if you try and play one through your home hi-fi without the accompanying 'digital vinyl system' technology, all you'll hear is an ear-piercing, high-pitched noise. So what's going on?

Let's start from the beginning. First of all, there's an argument to say that the development of 'digital vinyl systems' marked the biggest advance in DJ technology since Alex Rosner built a primitive three-channel mixer for Francis Grasso back in 1971. While there are now a multitude of ways to DJ digitally

– USB controllers, CD turntables and so on – when the first digital vinyl system was unveiled in 2001 it was years ahead of its time.

The genius of the system was that it

← Alongside friend and fellow techno DJ John Acquaviva, Richie Hawtin was an early adopter of the first 'digital vinyl system', Final Scratch
(Paxahau)

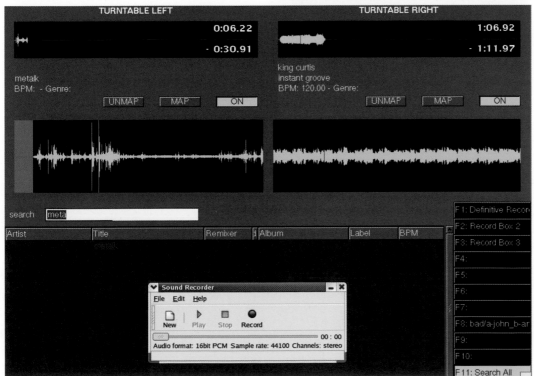

allowed DJs to perform using turntables, as they normally would. Yet the music they were playing was stored digitally on a portable hard drive or laptop. The people we have to thank for this innovation is a group of Dutch computer programmers, who stumbled onto the idea after seeing a DJ run out of records to play. To assist with the development of the pioneering system, they roped in two technology-savvy DJs: Canadian techno stars Richie Hawtin and John Acquaviva.

Since both Hawtin and Acquaviva were used to DJing with records, they demanded that the software could be controlled using regular turntables. Remarkably, the programmers managed to do it, and Final Scratch, the world's first 'digital vinyl system', was born.

The key to it all, of course, was their innovative 'timecode vinyl' design. For the system to be operational, users needed a pair of specially pressed timecode records, an audio interface called a 'scratch amp', and a DJing software application, Traktor Final Scratch, loaded onto a laptop. With this simple set-up, Hawtin and Acquaviva could mix any of the thousands of digital music files stored on their computers.

Positive peaks and negative valleys

From a DJ's perspective, the Final Scratch system was remarkably simple. Songs to be mixed in were assigned to the left or right turntable using the Traktor Final Scratch software application. Once a track had been assigned to a deck, it could then be played as if it were pressed into the grooves on the timecode control record. Press 'start' on the turntable, and the record would begin to play. If you stopped, pulled back or pushed forward the record by hand, the music would do just that, as if you were using a regular 12in record.

When the turntable's stylus was tracking the peaks and troughs pressed into the surface of the timecode record, it was actually tracking positive and negative voltages ('positive peaks' and 'negative valleys'). These were routed to the computer via the 'scratch amp' audio interface, which used an analogue-to-digital (ADC) converter to turn them into binary code (a constant stream of 'ones' and 'zeroes'). This code stream allowed the software to keep track of any changes in playback speed or direction.

So, if the DJ sped up the record using the turntable's pitch control function, the software would speed up its digital playback by the same amount. Similarly, if the DJ stopped the record, pulled it back or started doing scratch effects, the software would replicate this in playback.

The software was able to perform these acts of digital jiggery-pokery thanks to the way it handled any digital music files loaded into the software. Each file was analysed in order to assign a master tempo (in beats per minute, or 'BPM') and create a graphic representation of its sound waves. This was then displayed on screen to give DJs an additional visual aid to mixing, should the DJ decide to use it.

DJs were able to mix the files being played through the software application using their

regular DJ mixer. This is because the audio was routed to the mixer via the same 'scratch amp' audio interface that was used to receive control information.

Scratch that itch

Final Scratch pioneered the idea of synchronising the playback of stored audio files with control information fed to the computer via turntables and an audio interface. However, it wasn't long before rival systems, built on the same principles but subtly different, began appearing.

Today, there are numerous digital vinyl system (DVS) options for DJs to choose from. The most popular are Traktor Scratch (the direct descendant of Final Scratch) and Serato DJ, which is based on a system first launched in 2003, Serato Scratch Live. This was adopted by a large number of DJs throughout the noughties, who believed that its vinyl emulation was far more accurate than its rivals.

There are benefits to DVS other than mere vinyl emulation, though. Using the software, DJs can browse and arrange stored files by artist name, track title or tempo, create 'crates' – playlists, effectively – to group together tracks they want to play, and even insert 'cue points' within audio files. Most DVS applications also now include built-in special effects, looping, the ability to trigger audio samples using keyboard shortcuts, and integration with standalone 'DJ controller' hardware. You can find out more about the latter in Chapter 5.

⬇ Serato's Scratch Live system, developed with DJ equipment manufacturer Rane, helped to popularise the idea of DJing with turntables and a laptop computer

The art of vinyl

There's more to the appeal of vinyl than just the warm analogue sound of the records themselves. Artwork and packaging plays a big part too.

One of the most fascinating aspects of the recent 'vinyl revival' has been the willingness of record labels to pay more care and attention to the way their releases are presented and packaged. Today, even independent labels and small 'cottage' imprints – so-called because they're run out of someone's shed or record room – are willing to push the boat out, despite the increased costs of producing luscious artwork.

'I think kids are starting to look for something different as all they've grown up with is computer files,' says Paul Murphy, a graphic designer, musician and DJ who runs the acclaimed Claremont 56 label. 'Younger buyers are now getting interested in physical music formats. The packaging definitely helps with this. I get comments all the time about how much people treasure some of our releases. The fact that you can put it on a shelf or in a frame makes it much more of a valuable product.'

For those of a certain age, there's nothing novel about high-quality artwork and packaging. The look and feel of a record has always been part of its charm, for dedicated vinyl enthusiasts at the very least. For example, there's something particularly special about opening a gatefold sleeve to find detailed liner notes, song lyrics or unseen pictures of the band.

While it's always the music that matters, how a release is presented can enhance the listening experience, or at least give you a clue to the themes being explored by the musicians

→ Beautifully packaged box sets, such as this one from Claremont 56, are becoming an increasingly common sight in record shops, as record labels respond to the demand from vinyl enthusiasts for premium products

← Mark Farrow's design for Pet Shop Boys' 1988 dance album, *Introspective*, seemed to capture the loved-up feel of the times, combining a brilliantly simple outer cover with a vibrant and colourful inner sleeve featuring photographs of Chris Lowe and Neil Tennant

involved. Who hasn't at some point stared at the cover of an album while listening to it, trying to find clues within the image in front of them?

Iconic artwork

It's certainly true that many album covers have become almost as famous as the records themselves. Check, for example, the sublime simplicity of Georgie Hadie's cover for Pink Floyd's *Dark Side of the Moon*, the psychedelic brilliance of artist Peter Blake's work on The

↓ To help pay for the custom 'film canister' packaging used for the first 60,000 copies of their *Metal Box* album, Public Image Ltd were reportedly asked by Virgin Records to hand back a third of the 'advance' signing-on fee they'd been paid *(Ian Dunster)*

Beatles' *Sgt Pepper's Lonely Hearts Club Band* and the modified film canister created by Dennis Morris for Public Image Ltd's *Metal Box*.

All of these, along with countless other vinyl releases over the years, have become design classics. All in some way reflect the contents of the music contained within, or at the very least the designer's interpretation of the musicians' aural intentions. Over time, these images become intertwined with the music, just as certain music videos do, too (Michael Jackson's 'Thriller' and Aphex Twin's 'Come to Daddy' being obvious examples).

The use of a particular graphic designer can help define the visual identity of a band or record label, too. Check, for starters, the iconic purple 'house bags' created for techno and electronica label Warp Records by Ian Anderson of the Designers

↓ Many record labels, especially those whose releases are aimed at DJs, release singles in 'house bags' – customised card sleeves whose design will quickly become familiar to shoppers and listeners. This is a selection of Warp Records 'house bags' designed by Ian Anderson of the Designers Republic

Republic, or the distinctive look created for legendary Mancunian imprint Factory Records by Peter Saville.

Creating a visual identity

Paul Murphy's work for Claremont 56 would come under that bracket, too. Ever since he launched the label in 2007, Murphy has retained the same core elements – fonts, logos, spacing, colour combinations and so on – while working with a small pool of trusted artists and illustrators. As a result, it's easy to spot the label's releases in record stores.

'Most of the time I have a strong idea for the design from the first moment I hear the music,' Murphy says. 'I'll then either design it myself or brief another artist or designer on what I want. Occasionally the musicians involved will ask for a particular artist to be involved. If we go this way there is a certain look of the label that needs to be satisfied, so I retain some control over it.'

Since 2011, Murphy has worked extensively with illustrator Mark Warrington and his wife Emma March, who is also an experienced graphic designer. Both have played a role in helping his visual ideas come to life. 'When I first commissioned Mark to create an illustration for an album cover, I had a vision of a jungle,' Murphy remembers. 'I described it to him and he nailed it. After that commission, I have given Mark free rein to use his imagination and he's produced some beautiful pieces for me. His work has become synonymous with the look of the label.'

When it came to celebrating the label's tenth birthday in the summer of 2017, Murphy decided that he wanted to put out an extra-special release. He decided on a box set of previously unreleased music, featuring five slabs of wax (plus, on the more limited versions, a sixth 12in), housed in custom sleeves, inside an embossed, hand-numbered case. His vision was realised with a little help from his other half, Emma.

'She has great knowledge of paper stock and is fantastic with colours, so I started by describing what I wanted and then she made suggestions on what to use,' Murphy enthuses. 'She had a big part in design and a company she recommended built the boxes and did the foil stamping and embossing. Emma also picked the pantone colours that were used on the custom sleeves inside.'

The project took around six months to come to fruition, with Murphy and March exploring various options before deciding on the finished look. He believes it was worth it, though. 'The boxes are pretty bespoke and so cost a fortune by themselves, but it's an important part to get right as it's the first thing a customer sees and it needs to last, so should be strong yet beautiful,' Murphy insists. 'I wanted the inside to be minimal but Emma forced me to do the booklet with a foreword by a music journalist friend and tales from friends and label artists. Typography is my thing so I laid the type out and spent days copy-checking it over and over again. When the finished box sets turned up I was incredibly happy with the results.'

↓ Claremont 56's first box set, Originals 2008–2013, featured five records housed inside colour-coded gatefold sleeves

ECHOING THROUGH THE AGES

Over the years, many record sleeves have paid tribute to the artwork of classic or well-known album covers. Here are some of our favourite examples:

ELVIS PRESLEY – ELVIS PRESLEY (1956) / THE CLASH – LONDON CALLING (1979)

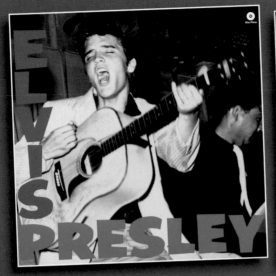 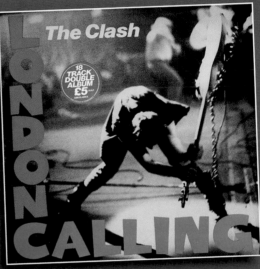

Elvis's debut album marked a significant landmark in the history of popular music, so it's perhaps unsurprising that a number of designers have paid tribute to the cover over the years. The most famous example is the cover of *London Calling* by The Clash, which subtly updates the design for the punk era. In hindsight, it looks less like a loving tribute to Elvis, and more of a dig at established rock culture.

Either way, the photo of Paul Simonon smashing up his bass guitar, shot by Pennie Smith at a gig in New York, has become one of music's most celebrated images.

PINK FLOYD – ATOM HEART MOTHER (1970) / THE KLF – CHILL OUT (1990)

When commissioning cover art for their 1970 set *Atom Heart Mother*, Pink Floyd asked design collective Hipgnosis for 'something plain'. They duly delivered, opting for a gatefold that featured a picture of a cow grazing and no explanatory text. Two decades later, dance music mavericks The KLF delivered their spin on the design for the cover of ambient house album *Chill Out,* replacing the cow with grazing sheep.

Associated act The Orb later paid tribute to both *Chill Out* and the cover of another Floyd album, *Animals*, on the sleeve of *Live '93*.

The weird world of vinyl

Second-hand store owner Michael Savage has seen a lot of weird, wonderful and downright odd records pass through his shop over the years. We asked him to highlight some of the strangest.

↓ **While sorting through second-hand records he's bought in bulk, Mike Savage often comes across releases that are unusual at best**

Of the tens of millions of records that have been released over the last decade, only a relatively small number are any good. Yet it's always these that are celebrated, rather than the odd, awful and ill-advised.

Mike Savage, owner of the Prime Cuts second-hand store in Bristol, England, has a passion for these kinds of hard-to-explain records – or, more specifically, the undeniably terrible artwork that many are accompanied by. In a bid to celebrate vinyl culture's eccentric margins, we asked Mike to showcase some of the stranger records that have passed through his shop over the years.

Nigel Yoxon & Mark Bailey – The Soundbusters

We're not sure we want to hear the covers of 'He Ain't Heavy (He's My Brother)' and 'Ave Maria' featured on the sole album from Nigel Yoxon and Mark Bailey. Their version of 'The Dambusters Theme' is probably a bit of a banger, though.

Mike Savage: 'We can only hope that Nigel and Mark weren't sucked into the propellers moments after the cover picture was taken.'

Unknown Artist – Top of the Tots Pop Party

Disturbingly, this monstrosity was part of a series of Top of the Tots 'soundalike' compilations aimed at children. We shudder to think how bad the music actually is.

Mike Savage: 'Proof that the 1970s were pretty shit, really.'

The Fureys & Davey Arthur – Golden Days

Sibling Irish folk band The Fureys recorded a large number of albums with friend Davey Arthur during the late 1970s and early '80s. Almost all feature artwork as bad as this.

Mike Savage: 'I think this is officially the most depressing sleeve artwork ever. It's also unrealistic, as the dog would be trying to attack those ducks.'

Acker Bilk, His Clarinet & Strings – Invitation...

The legendary clarinettist and bandleader released an astonishing number of easy-listening albums in the '60s and '70s. This is not among his best.

Mike Savage: 'Acker seems to be channelling Robert De Niro. Raging Bilk.'

Various Artists – Disco Flyer

During the disco boom of the 1970s, record labels released countless cash-in compilations like this one. Most, though not all, featured cover art as bad as this.

Mike Savage: 'This super disco lady needs to cheer up a bit. Maybe she misses her home world?'

Doctor Keith Cammeron – Live With Love

If you're encountering problems in the bedroom, Doctor Keith Cammeron could help. Alternatively, his words of wisdom could make them worse.

Mike Savage: 'Those massive bees would probably spoil the intimacy of the moment.'

Bryan Smith & His Happy Piano – Back in Your Own Backyard

We're a little disturbed by Bryan Smith's 'backyard', which appears to be set inside a Cold War nuclear bunker. His piano doesn't look all that happy, either.

Mike Savage: 'Bryan's place sure looks inviting.'

Ena Baga – Salute to Al Jolson and Fats Waller

During the Second World War, the exotically named Ena Baga was the resident organist at the Tower Ballroom. Here she's paying tribute to two American greats in the only way she knows how. Yep, by getting out her Hammond Concorde.

Mike Savage: 'This is a typeface pile-up.'

David Price – Tune Tonic

If you've ever wondered what a banjo interpretation of Chopin would sound like, track down this 'recital' by David Price. Be warned, though: the music is predictably as bad as the cover artwork.

Mike Savage: 'This just says "fun" to me.'

Ken Goodwin – Settle Down With Ken Goodwin

To be fair, Ken's living room does look rather inviting. We'd happily share a glass of brandy with him, provided we didn't have to listen to any of his music.

Mike Savage: 'Note that Ken is rocking the one-sock look here. Bold move.'

Caring for your records

Vinyl rewards rough treatment with pops and crackles – best avoided. Here are our top tips for keeping your cherished record collection in pristine condition.

Vinyl records may look and sound great, but they take far more looking after than CDs or a hard drive full of digital music files. To ensure years of happy playback and solid sound quality, periodic care and attention should be paid not only to the surface of the disc itself, but also to how you handle and store your records.

Handling records the right way

The first thing to learn is how to handle records. Unless you're a DJ, where touching the playing area is essential during the mixing process, you should try and refrain from putting your fingers on the surface at any point. Greasy marks are not just an eyesore, but the grease can also

↓ When holding vinyl, remember to keep your fingertips off the playing surface

potentially get into the grooves and reduce sound quality. In theory, if there's anything corrosive on your fingers – detergents, acids, and so on – then the damage could be irrecoverable.

So, what's the best method for taking records in and out of sleeves? Holding the spine of the sleeve in one hand, gently slip the record out so that the round edge of the disc is supported by the palm of your other hand, as shown in the picture on the left.

Once it's half out of its protective sheath, feel free to place a fingertip or two underneath the disc, making sure that you only touch the printed centre label. Fingerprint marks can mess with the artwork, too, so don't keep them there too long. As soon as the record is fully removed from the sleeve, carefully hold it in two hands, with the edges resting in your palms. There's an example 'best practice' photo on the previous page for guidance.

Staving off static build-up

While fingermarks are annoying, dust and static build-up – which, irritatingly, then attracts more dust – are the record collector's real enemy. There are a few things you can do to reduce the build-up of both of these tiny terrors.

For starters, storing your records in polythene-lined paper inners, rather than the cheaper paper versions, cuts down on static build-up. These can be bought in bulk fairly cheaply from online retailers, and they really do help to reduce static build-up.

Another neat trick to reduce the build-up of static, and the dust that it attracts, is to gently

← The Discovery One Redux is the ultimate cleaner: it uses a 'medical grade' pump to remove all deposits, restoring the vinyl to near-factory condition *(Keith Monks Audio Works)*

brush the surface of the record before and after playback. Suitable brushes are available from many record shops as well as specialist dealers and only cost a few pounds. We're not lying when we say it's worth the investment.

Keep it clean

However well you look after your records, it's inevitable that dust will find its way in to the grooves. Because of this, regular cleaning is recommended. Now, there are numerous ways to do this, both for those on a budget and those with plenty of cash to spare.

If you're willing to part with a few hundred pounds (or dollars), then we'd suggest opting for a motorised Record Cleaning Machine (RCM). These big beasts vary in size, design and price, but most look remarkably similar to old-fashioned record players. There is one big difference, though: instead of having a tonearm, RCMs boast a tonearm-shaped vacuum that aggressively sucks hard-to-shift dust off the surface of the record. It's a neat trick and really works, though a decent one could set you back more than you paid for your turntable.

If a vinyl Hoover is out of your price range, manual alternatives are available. These cheaper Record Cleaning Machines are operated by hand and involve rotating the record through a liquid bath of water and record cleaning solution. The damp record can then be dried and hand-cleaned with a microfibre cloth or velvet brush.

If you don't fancy acquiring an automatic or manual RCM, you should at least purchase a bottle of decent vinyl-cleaning solution (which is dribbled or sprayed on to the surface of the record) and a microfibre cloth. You might have to make a few attempts to remove all of the dust and grime – especially on a record that's not had much attention for a while – but this method will still do a solid job.

VINYL CARE DOS & DON'TS

DO
- ■ Keep records away from direct sunlight
- ■ Ensure that your record room or storage space is free of excess moisture (too much water in the air can lead to mould)
- ■ Clean second-hand records before playing them for the first time
- ■ Put records back into sleeves after playback
- ■ Use the turntable's dust cover (that's the plastic lid) if it has one, especially when you're not using the deck

DON'T
- ■ Store records close to heat sources such as radiators and fireplaces
- ■ Touch the tonearm, head shell or stylus during playback – this can lead to scratches that will permanently damage the records
- ■ Put anything corrosive on the record's surface – only use specialist record cleaning solution
- ■ Leave records sat on the turntable platter for extended periods of time
- ■ Allow records to lie around outside sleeves, gathering dust

Chapter Four

Vinyl culture

(Shutterstock)

Shop 'til you drop

The ins and outs of acquiring records, from major high-street retailers to specialist stores, second-hand shops and online options.

↓ London's LoveVinyl store, which stocks both new releases and second-hand wax, is widely considered to be one of the best record shops in the UK *(Paul Marshall Photography)*

For many vinyl enthusiasts, there's nothing more pleasurable than whiling away a few hours flicking through racks of records. Whether you're idly browsing or hunting for something specific, time quickly ebbs away while you read the small print, inspect the surface of the record or make your way through the liner notes. It's a ritual that has been an important part of many music fans' lives for years or decades.

Sadly, the days of there being a record shop on every high street are long gone, and those independent outlets that have survived often do as much business online as they do from store visitors. Even so, the record-retailing scene is in a more healthy state than it has been for many years. What's more, there are more options for record-hungry buyers than ever before. So, without further ado, here's our guide to the 21st-century record shopping experience.

High-street chains

Branches of music chain stores such as HMV and Our Price were once a familiar sight on British high streets. Even those towns that didn't boast one at least had a Woolworths store that sold albums and singles amongst the assorted pic 'n' mix, toys and stationery.

Today, the number of music chain stores has reduced dramatically, though those that survive usually stock vinyl in their bigger stores. 'Woollies' is long gone, of course, but thanks to the vinyl revival, some other large retailers such as Tesco and Urban Outfitters do sometimes stock a small selection of records.

Unfortunately, even a relatively large branch of, say, HMV or Fopp will still only stock a very limited range of new releases, compilations and reissues. This is, of course, fine if you're looking for the latest Coldplay album, but not so good if you're on the hunt for obscure underground music.

Independent stores and specialists

Here we're talking about retailers that either stock a wide range of new releases and back catalogue stock – including both mainstream or underground releases – or outlets that specialise in certain types of music, such as DJ-friendly dance music shops.

In these places, staff members are invariably also massive vinyl nerds. While some may look moody and unapproachable, they're usually more than happy to chat music and recommend records to listen to on their dedicated listening posts (aka a turntable and a pair of headphones).

Independent and specialist outlets are often the beating heart of the underground music community in the town or city in which they're based. These shops are as much a meeting place for DJs and local record collectors as somewhere to flick through boxes of new releases. In this way, they're far more significant

to the health of alternative music scenes than many give them credit for.

Second-hand shops

Often dusty, dark, eccentric and run by miserable record collectors who were once happy to make a living out of their hobby, these stores specialise in used records. The owners, who often also sell stock at record fairs or through online marketplaces, usually have a deep knowledge of music and the desirability or otherwise of particular records. Second-hand stores are alluring to obsessive vinyl hoarders, principally because you never know what you might find.

Sometimes, you'll find a clean copy of a long-sought-after gem at a reasonable price, at others 24 scuffed copies of well-known records

by Prince, Tears for Fears or the Rolling Stones. On rare occasions, you'll spot a cracking 12in or album in the bargain boxes that would usually go for a much higher price online.

Websites for buying and selling vinyl have impacted on the second-hand stores in a number of ways. Some stores now survive primarily by selling their stock online, while other owners base their prices on what records are listed for on particular 'vinyl marketplaces'. You'll have to pay the asking price unless you can haggle with the shop owner. If you're buying multiple records, it's not unusual for counter staff to give you a discount (especially if you've selected records that they've been trying to shift for years).

Mail order websites

What could be more convenient than sitting on your sofa and shopping for records? That's the basic premise behind mail order websites, which often stock a far wider range of new releases

than your average local record shop. Many are based in industrial units or warehouses, stock an impressive range of back catalogue items and order more copies of essential new releases than smaller retailers (making them a good option if you're searching for records that have been pressed in limited quantities).

There's no denying that using these kinds of online outlets is nowhere near as satisfying as buying from local record shops – you have to wait for your purchases to arrive through the mail, after all – but they are convenient. The best online stores, such as Juno Records, pay a lot of attention to customer service, sending out completed orders the same day where possible. Even so, there's nothing like being able to chat with a fellow vinyl enthusiast while browsing through records, which is something you won't get from online outlets.

Online marketplaces

Even those with little interest in records will have used online auction site eBay at some point. Ever since it launched in the mid-1990s, furious bidding wars have broken out between record collectors over desirable releases. There's nothing like the feeling of elation when your bid comes out tops, though the feeling of regret when you realise you have paid over the odds is similarly memorable.

These days, many collectors prefer to use Discogs Marketplace instead. This is the online store of the popular Discogs.com music database. Literally anyone can sign up to buy or sell records on Discogs; sellers pay a small commission fee for

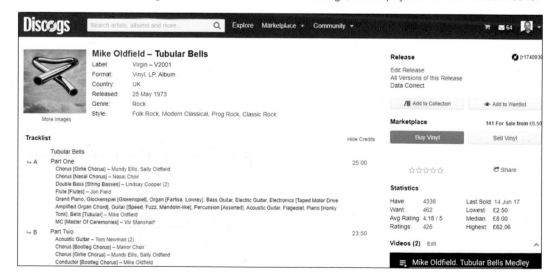

← More than 500 dealers and tens of thousands of vinyl enthusiasts at Record Planet in Utrecht, Netherlands

every item sold, whereas buyers must pay postage on top of the cost of each record bought. Sellers are expected to honestly grade their records based on the same system used by record dealers (mint, near mint, very good and so on). Unlike eBay, there's no bidding involved: sellers set the price, and the buyer has to decide whether it's one they're willing to pay.

If you're after obscure, hard-to-find or rare items, the Discogs marketplace is a great place to start. If there's a record you've been trying to track down for years, there's a good chance there will be at least one copy for sale on Discogs. It might cost you more than you'd like, but that's supply and demand for you.

Record fairs

Long before the Internet made searching for and buying records an easy pursuit, record fairs were a collector's dream. Usually held in large halls, fairs featured stalls from record dealers who were looking to shift as much of their second-hand stock as possible. Today, the number and frequency of record fairs is naturally lower, but there are still plenty held across the UK, Europe and beyond. As with second-hand shops, you can sometimes haggle over prices with sellers, and the best fairs include stalls from dealers specialising in different kinds of music (classic rock, dance music, soul, jazz and so on). These days, there are some seriously sizeable fairs for record-hungry collectors to attend. The biggest annual event takes place at a Conference Centre in Utrecht in the Netherlands, and features over 500 different sellers. For any vinyl enthusiast with deep pockets, it's a must-attend event.

RECORD SHOP ETIQUETTE

In an attempt to create more harmonious relations between shoppers and record store staff, we asked Jake Holloway of London's LoveVinyl to give us some tips to guarantee a more pleasurable shopping experience. Here's his top dos and don'ts for customers…

DO

■ **Respect the vinyl**
'Handle with care, always hold the record by its edges and replace it in its inner sleeve and cover properly.'
■ **Give yourself plenty of time**
'It's a process. Only take a boyfriend or girlfriend if they love digging through racks of records, too.'
■ **Check the new arrivals section**
'The new releases racks in shops such as LoveVinyl are often topped up throughout the day, as new stock arrives. Diggers in the know head to this section first.'

DON'T

■ **Check prices of records online**
'Don't do this in full view of the staff. If you feel the need to sneakily check Discogs prices for comparison purposes, at least be inconspicuous about it.'
■ **Listen to a record unless you intend to buy**
'You're in a record shop, not a library. It's unfair to other paying customers to listen to records you have no intention of purchasing.'
■ **Ask for a discount**
'Discounts are given to those who earn their stripes. You might be offered a discount, but it's rude to ask – especially if you're visiting a store for the first time.'

The record clubs

Fancy getting a box of hand-picked records delivered to your door every month? If so, you'll need to join a vinyl subscription service. We asked the experts at *What Hi-Fi?* to pick out eight of the best.

Until the vinyl revival kicked in a few years back, the days of the 'record clubs' – subscription services that delivered fresh releases and exclusive items to your door every month – seemed numbered. Happily, renewed interest in vinyl culture has seen a boom in subscription services catering for all kinds of musical tastes.

In all honesty, when we started researching this list, we were surprised by how many credible vinyl subscription services are out there. But they all share one aspect, whether it be mixing LPs with beer or wine, pressing exclusive records or playing the role of record-store-manager-cum-sonic-guru: these are all services you can't replicate simply by clicking through 'related artists' on Spotify. So, without further ado, here are eight of the best record subscription services around....

(Vinyl Moon)

Hurd

http://wearehurd.co.uk
What you get: One 7in single and four craft beers or craft ciders
Price: £17.99–19.99 per month

We can think of nothing finer than supping an obscure craft beer or cider whilst listening to a brand new record. Happily, Hurd is a service for similarly minded people. Each month, subscribers receive a coloured 7in single from an emerging artist (usually from within the indie and alternative scene, but they do vary it a little), plus four bottles of beer or cider (or a mix of both) from little-known microbreweries around the UK and Europe. The box also contains the service's own music-and-beer-centric periodical and an extra piece of limited-edition merchandise.

Wax & Stamp

www.waxandstamp.com
What you get: One LP and one 7in EP a month
Price: £28 per month (additional shipping fees apply outside the UK)

According to Wax & Stamp's website, founders Luke and Josh were inspired to start the service because they missed getting recommendations from record shop staff. Each month they select one record and invite a guest to pick the other. So far, guests have included snooker legend Steve Davis, author Bill Brewster and comedian Josie Long, as well as various DJs and label managers, and genres covered have been as varied as post-dubstep and Spanish garage rock.

Flying Vinyl

www.flyingvinyl.co.uk
What you get: Five exclusive 7in singles plus artist info booklet
Price: £20 per month

Each of Flying Vinyl's monthly boxes contains 7in singles featuring the best new indie, alternative and rock tracks discovered by the music enthusiast behind the service, Craig Evans. The featured tracks tend to be vinyl exclusives, with each individual 7in boasting its own custom-designed artwork. You also get an info booklet on the featured artists, giving background on any you've never heard of, and there's sometimes an extra treat thrown in (past boxes have included stickers, Polaroids and exclusive prints).

Vinyl Moon

www.vinylmoon.co

What you get: A 10-track compilation LP of handpicked new bands

Price: $37-$39/month (including international shipping fees)

If you're after new musical recommendations, but a little tentative about putting all your trust into one picked-out artist, Vinyl Moon swerves the risk by putting together a rather eclectic mix tape, pressing it to coloured vinyl and commissioning a visual artist to design the cover - so you end up with something entirely individual. As with most of these discovery-based services, you also get relevant literature to tell you about the bands you're listening to, as well as lyric sheets and individual artwork for each track. A set of postcards to spread the word about the acts you like is another pleasant flourish.

Stylus

www.stylusvinyl.com

What you get: A classic album with specially commissioned 12 x 12in art piece, a bottle of wine and Stylus's own magazine

Price: £25 per month (without wine), £35 per month (with wine)

This is really one for those beginning a collection, who want to include all the albums BBC Four have probably made a documentary about. We're talking *Rumours* by Fleetwood Mac and Prince's *Purple Rain*, records the majority of people who want them already have. Selected by a musician and food writer named Russ and his wife, the rest of your box's contents make sense: a bottle of wine chosen by award-winning merchant Great Western Wine, and a magazine including interviews with musicians and winemakers (as well as tasting and listening notes).

The Retro Store

http://theretro.co.uk

What you get: Three 'mystery' second-hand albums every month

Price: £15 per month

Not everybody enjoys hours spent rummaging in record shops and taking a chance on an eye-catching cover, so the Retro Store offers to do all that for you. You can let them know the kind of music you're into and they'll try to match your tastes, or allow them full licence to expand your sonic horizons. The company doesn't deal solely in vinyl – it offers similar services for cassettes, games and comics, too – but it's their wax subscription service that interests us. Living in the past rarely seems so appealing.

Feedbands

https://feedbands.com/vinyl

What you get: A first pressing of the monthly record, with digital download and lyric sheet or art print

Price: $20 per month (plus shipping fees)

Easily among our top picks on this list, Feedbands' concept is a community-based vehicle for getting independent artists' albums their first pressing. Anyone, from anywhere in the world, can upload their music – either a full album or a bunch of tracks from which Feedbands can make a compilation. Anyone signed up to the site, which is free, can then vote for their favourite songs and those with a decent number of votes – typically 125+ across an artist's uploaded tracks – has the chance of being pressed and sent out to each subscriber. What's more, if you don't like any month's record you can swap it for anything that isn't sold out from the catalogue.

Trax & Wax

www.traxnwax.com

What you get: Two or four DJ-friendly 12in singles per month, depending on which plan you opt for

Price: £21.90 (two records) / £36.90 (four records) per month

Trax & Wax is a subscription service for DJs and dance music enthusiasts, delivering a fresh batch of currently hot 12in singles to your door each month. There are six genre-specific boxes to choose from – 'Trax & Wax' (house and deep house), disco, 'old school' (house and techno reissues), 'nu school' (tech-house), techno, and drum & bass – and you can switch between them as you wish. Their selections are usually spot-on and include must-have club hits, future underground anthems and great records you may have missed.

An introduction to 'crate digging'

The most obsessive record collectors often go to extreme lengths to find records. This is 'crate digging': the art of sniffing out killer records, sometimes in the most unlikely of places.

If you've ever found a sought-after record for 50 pence at a charity shop, or discovered a secret stash of albums for sale in the back of a barbershop in Sydney, then you can class yourself as an apprentice 'crate digger'. If you haven't, but spend much of your spare time visiting new places on the off chance of stumbling on a haul of vinyl gold, then you also fit the bill.

Really, though, anyone can become a crate digger. All it takes is a burning passion for vinyl, an extensive and detailed knowledge of music (or just one or two particular styles of music) and the dedication to spend most of your spare time flicking through the contents of dusty boxes of old records.

⬇ **Zaf, one of the co-owners of London's LoveVinyl store, is highly regarded in record collecting circles thanks to his knack of finding obscure and sought-after records** (*Paul Marshall Photography*)

'mined' by other diggers, so locating potential sources of records in smaller places can often bear fruit.

Some serious 'diggers' think nothing of travelling overseas on record hunting missions, either. The most committed, some of which are profiled later in this chapter (Mining the past: the rise of the record collector DJs), often head to a particular country or city on a hunch. While there, they will talk to locals to see whether they know of any secret stashes of records hidden in lock-ups, garages, shipping containers or former record distribution warehouses. It may sound like a long shot, but if they're lucky their persistence will pay off and they'll uncover something truly rare and magical.

This is, of course, dedication beyond the call of duty. Those who take this approach tend to be those who intend to make a living out of it; either music producers who are searching for weird and wonderful records to sample when making their own records, or dealers on the lookout for releases that they can clean up and sell on for a tidy profit.

↑ Serious crate diggers are happy to spend many hours searching through each box or rack of records in a dusty second-hand store like this one

➜ You don't necessarily need to plan a dedicated record-hunting holiday to 'dig' abroad. Instead, be on the lookout for flea markets and record shops while on family holidays

Where to dig

Serious crate diggers are always looking for opportunities to find records. That means countless visits to yard sales, car boot sales, flea markets, charity shops and thrift stores, as well as trips to other towns and cities. Often, second-hand stores and charity shops in sizeable towns and cities have already been

How to dig

The number one rule of crate digging is always to keep your eyes open for boxes of records,

wherever they may be. Ninety-nine times out of a hundred, you'll struggle to find anything other than long-forgotten 7in singles of dreadful pop hits, but your effort is rewarded when you spot something from your 'wants list' languishing amongst a box of BBC sound effects records and unwanted copies of terrible novelty albums.

As ever, knowledge is key. Know your subject matter inside out and what you're looking for. The greater your knowledge, the more likely you'll be able to fathom out whether mystery records might be quite good. Liner credits – musicians, producers, record label and year of production – should be studied carefully for clues. Of course, that might not make it a great or even hard-to-find record, but it will at least give you a clue as to the record's contents (and whether you should take a punt on it). Remember: if you buy something for a bargain price and it turns out to be a stinker, you can always quietly drop it off in your local charity shop and forget your mistake.

It's always worth remembering that not all owners of charity shops or second-hand stores know all that much about records. While it's becoming more common for counter staff to consult online sites such as

Discogs Marketplace when pricing up stock, some just don't have the time to do this. Therefore, they throw unfamiliar records into crates of 'bargain' records with the same standardised price (think a pound or a dollar, as an example). If you're lucky, you might find something valuable, or simply really good, hidden in one of these boxes.

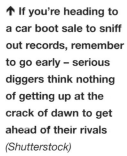

↑ If you're heading to a car boot sale to sniff out records, remember to go early – serious diggers think nothing of getting up at the crack of dawn to get ahead of their rivals *(Shutterstock)*

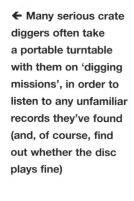

← Many serious crate diggers often take a portable turntable with them on 'digging missions', in order to listen to any unfamiliar records they've found (and, of course, find out whether the disc plays fine)

The world's most valuable vinyl

Even if your collection boasts some rare gems, it's unlikely any will be quite as sought-after as these exceedingly rare records. Welcome to the world of auctions, acetates and one-offs.

↑ When rare records come up for auction they often sell for far more than the catalogue list price, as rich collectors battle it out to secure a piece of history (Sotheby's)

→ Ringo Starr's 2015 auction of precious Beatles-related memorabilia raised millions of dollars for the charity he established with his wife, the Lotus Foundation
(Eva Rinaldi)

In December 2015, some of the world's richest collectors of music memorabilia gathered at Julien's, Los Angeles, for one of the most eagerly anticipated charity auctions of all time.

Amongst the lots was a treasure trove of unique items owned by Ringo Starr, including a Ludwig drum kit used by the drummer in over 200 Beatles concerts, his suit from the band's first film, *A Hard Day's Night*, and electric guitars once owned by John Lennon and George Harrison.

For many of the gathered collectors, there was only one item that they must bid on: Ringo's copy of 1968 double-album *The Beatles*, more commonly known as *The White Album*. When the album was first released, every vinyl copy was numbered. The one Ringo was selling, thought to have initially been gifted to John Lennon, bore the number 0000001, making it the first copy to roll off the presses.

Low-numbered copies of *The White Album* had previously changed hands for big sums of money. In 2008, an album numbered 0000005 sold at auction for £23,500 ($30,000); given the uniqueness of Ringo's copy, the record was expected to go for double that when it finally came up for auction.

In the end, the winning bid was an astonishing £620,400 ($790,000), making the 'mint condition' rarity, which Starr had kept in a vault for the previous 35 years, officially the most expensive record ever sold at auction.

Ace acetates

The astonishing price achieved by Ringo's copy of *The White Album* is a reflection not only of its worth to Beatles collectors, but also its undoubted rarity. For the most part, records

→ **Paul McCartney's 10in acetate featuring early recordings of the Quarrymen is naturally one of the most sought-after records amongst dedicated Beatles collectors** (Beatlesource)

that fetch ridiculously high sums at auction tend to be genuine 'one-offs'.

For example, in January 2015, Jack White of the White Stripes parted with a staggering £232,000 ($300,000) to purchase a 10in, 78rpm acetate cut by Elvis Presley's management in 1953. Featuring Presley's cover of a 1948 song called 'My Happiness', the acetate is undoubtedly of historic interest. The song was recorded during The King's first session at Sun Studios in Memphis and marked his first appearance on vinyl, almost 12 months before his debut single, 'That's All Right', was released.

Acetates, which are one-off test records created for demonstration or evaluation purposes are, by their very nature, rare items. When the artists involved are of interest to a large number of collectors, their value sky-rockets. The band that later became the Beatles, the Quarrymen, recorded two songs ('That'll Be the Day' and early McCartney/Harrison composition 'In Spite of All the Danger') at an electrical shop in Liverpool in 1958. The band members cobbled together enough money to press up one 78rpm, 10in acetate.

Since then, this unique chunk of Beatles history has been in the possession of Paul McCartney. Its value has been estimated at well over £200,000 by *Record Collector* magazine, despite the recordings being widely bootlegged (and later included on the first *Beatles Anthology* compilation). Intriguingly, legitimate 'replica' copies do exist, as McCartney got a small number (25 10in acetates, 25 7in singles) pressed up in 1981 as Christmas gifts to friends and family. Even these are estimated to be worth at least £10,000 each.

One of a kind

Some artists recognise the value amongst collectors of genuinely one-off items. In 1983, French star Jean-Michel Jarre recorded an album's worth of music for an art exhibition. He decided to treat what became *Music for*

Supermarkets as a work of art in its own right. One copy of the album was pressed at the MPO manufacturing plant and put up for auction. At the auction, both the master tapes and the 'mother' record created to press the lone album were destroyed. Jarre's ultra-limited edition was bought for 69,000 Francs (roughly equivalent to €10,500); today, it is estimated to be worth between £20,000 and £30,000 ($26,000–$39,000).

← If you have £25,000 spare, you could own one of the three known surviving copies of Frank Wilson's Northern Soul anthem 'Do I Love You (Indeed I Do)' *(Discogs)*

were destroyed. Nobody knows exactly how many copies of the record have survived, though soul collectors know of three (only two of which are playable).

The record's infamy is due, in part, to the way it was 'rediscovered' in the Motown archives in 1977. The label's sole copy was then 'borrowed' by a researcher, who allowed a friend to create a small number of acetate copies. These were then sent to Northern Soul DJs in the UK, who began playing them at such legendary venues as the Wigan Casino and the Blackpool Mecca.

A year later, a British DJ named Jonathan Woodliffe acquired the original Motown library copy via a record dealer for £250 – a staggering amount of money for a record in 1978. A year later, he exchanged it with fellow Northern Soul DJ and vinyl trader Kev Roberts for £350 worth of records. Woodliffe may now be regretting his decision; in 2009, another original copy of the rare 7in single sold for over £25,000 at auction to an 'unnamed bidder'. There has naturally been much speculation about the identity of the bidder, with many soul collectors speculating that it was none other than Frank Wilson himself.

Of course, not all valuable records are those made by well-known and successful musicians, though prices do tend to be higher if demand amongst collectors is high. One of the most sought-after 1960s soul records of all time was not made by one of Motown's best-known names, but rather an obscure singer/songwriter – and later record producer – called Frank Wilson.

In 1965, Wilson recorded a single for one of Motown's sub-labels entitled 'Do I Love You (Indeed I Do)'. Neither Wilson nor Motown boss Berry Gordy were happy with it, so all but a handful of the 250 promotional 7in singles the label manufactured

← Due to popular demand, Tamla Motown reissued 'Do I Love You (Indeed I Do)' on 7in single in 1979. Copies of this pressing currently fetch a more modest £60–90, putting it within the budget of most record collectors

Meet the record dealer

Today, more people around the world are making a living buying and selling records than ever before. Markus Holler, a 25-year veteran of the art, tells us how it works.

'You have to remember that vinyl never went away. When CDs and digital took over, guys like us were still selling vinyl and it went for serious money.' So says Markus Holler, owner of Sugarbush Records in Tunbridge Wells, Kent, who is one of many thousands of entrepreneurs worldwide who make a living by trading vinyl from their homes.

To make the point, Markus finds an article in the *Financial Times* that quotes him in 2006 talking about vinyl as an area of investment alongside wine, art and classic cars. Back then, when it was difficult to know how rare a pressing was, he could sell an album by King Crimson or Black Sabbath for three figures, despite it being relatively easy to find. 'Russian collectors hit the market 10 to 12

↓ Markus Holler amongst the stock of second-hand records he sells to record collectors around the world

↑ **Like all record dealers, Markus Holler inspects the records he's selling in order to grade their quality. Unblemished 'mint' or 'near-mint' records naturally fetch more than those riddled with dust and scratches**

years ago but they didn't really know what the prices were,' says Holler, 'and that made values sky-rocket.'

It all began in the early 1990s when, as a sound engineer, Markus tried selling records in the specialist audio shop where he worked in Richmond, Surrey. Vinyl was fast disappearing from the high street and, soon after, he saw the opportunity to start a standalone business.

'I had an epiphany. CD was taking over and people were selling their vinyl for nothing,' he enthuses. 'I borrowed some money from my dad and started to buy and sell, getting stock from car boot sales and record fairs and advertising in the classifieds in *Loot*.'

Trading places dealer

Markus now has 20,000 LPs and singles in stock, of which about 40% are catalogued. 'There could be great stuff in the 13,000 I haven't listed yet,' he says, pointing to a stack of big see-through plastic boxes. 'There will be £300 albums in those boxes. I need to get around to it.'

→ **Copies of Markus's catalogue of stock for sale, which are mailed to regular customers and record collectors the world over**

What's the vinyl trading sector like? 'They are all enthusiasts and very knowledgeable. It can be a bit geeky. People have been known to collect by catalogue number and reference numbers etched into the runout groove. But I was never into that – there's money in it, but it's too scientific for me.'

The customers are highly diverse. Some just want to own the rare stuff, buying a track because of its value rather than because they like the music. Holler has got to know a wide range of people over the years, including someone who only collected greatest hits albums, regardless of music genre, or another who just wanted copies of the Beatles' *White Album*, which has a unique number on each copy. But the advent of the web, and in particular the online trading platform Discogs, has meant a more automated process where customer interactions are less frequent – although it has opened his business up to international markets, which now account for two-thirds of his sales.

Discogs, the 'Wikipedia for records', now handles the majority of his stock, replacing the unloved eBay which had a uniform approach to selling rather than an experience that is tuned to vinyl. Discogs has helped him to sell more types of music and he is less of a specialist as a result. 'A guy from China last week spent £450 on modern stoner rock – that would never have happened in the old days.'

The continuing hunt for vinyl

Despite all that, Holler still produces a print catalogue and spends hours at the wheel of his Volvo 850 estate visiting private sellers and record fairs. 'Buying is much more fun than selling,' he says. 'I got a call from a guy who was trying to sell his collection to a well-known shop in Soho for months but they were too busy. I went up to his lockup the same week and found 4,000 records, all mint, and you could tell the phases he went through in his music life. The first one I sold was Joy Division's *An Ideal for Living*, which went the next day for £1,300 and got my money back. I did six months' work in a day.'

His biggest-ever return to date has been an eponymous prog rock LP by Motiffe on Deroy Records from 1972, which he sold recently for

↑ **Markus struck gold when he found this rare acetate copy of the Beatles' 'Get Back', backed with 'Don't Let Me Down', in the archive of a deceased record collector**

£2,000. On an estimated purchase price of £3 in 1972, that's an annual return of 16 per cent over 45 years, although most records will have changed hands frequently over that timespan.

Holler has also released a number of records under his independent label, using one of the three big European factories that still press vinyl, GZ in the Czech Republic (eagle-eyed readers may remember that this colossal establishment was also featured earlier in the book). A former communist pressing plant, it managed to survive the lean years.

'Vinyl repressing never went away and there were big volumes of re-releases even ten years ago,' Markus says. 'Dance vinyl kept the presses going and, as digital took over and it moved away, everything else ramped up. The quality is right up there.'

Holler is always on the lookout for something collectable and has a sizeable personal collection that he 'would never sell', which he uses at a disco and soul night he runs with an ex-pro DJ at the Forum in Tunbridge Wells.

A good example of a record that could be a hidden gem is the original red label of *Please Please Me* by the Beatles, an instant £150. But if it's a black label with gold lettering, then that could be £5,000.

'You never know what you are going to find. I bought an old box of 7in singles for £20 last month and there was a Beatles acetate in a wrong sleeve. It was unique and worth £1,000.' Which is why, says Holler, he's never going to stop.

BLAME IT ON THE BOOGIE

Stick the words 'vinyl' and 'night' into Facebook and you will get a long, long list of events all around the world, from Nashville to Minnesota to Pensacola. Dig a bit deeper and you will come to Boogie Nights, a monthly funk, disco and hip-hop night at The Forum in Tunbridge Wells, Kent, a converted Victorian public lavatory once voted the *NME*'s best small music venue. Behind the decks you will find Richard Marshall, a former professional DJ, alongside Markus Holler.

'I have been buying, collecting and playing vinyl since the 1970s. When I left uni, a mate and I set up our own record shop called Funky World in Stafford,' says Richard. 'I also began producing my own tracks using an Akai S950, one of the early samplers that made the dance music revolution possible.'

He kept DJing and producing until his big break in 1999, when Norman Cook, aka Fatboy Slim, signed his track 'Because of You' under the guise of Scanty Sandwich, to his Southern Fried label. 'I made that track in about four hours in the studio using a Michael Jackson sample, which amazingly we got clearance on – apparently he had to approve it personally.' It went to number three in the UK charts and made it on to *Top of the Pops*.

Richard went on to DJ professionally for five years, supporting Fatboy Slim numerous times all over the world, stopping only when his wife Becca gave birth to their son in 2004. Although not completely stopping: Richard launched Boogie Nights two years ago. 'We get such a great crowd – people of all ages and musical tastes. They love the tunes and they love that it's all on vinyl – and it's still exciting to mix two tracks, live, to 300 people.'

← **Richard Marshall on a tour of Russia in the early 2000s: the sign says 'Scanty Sandwich'. Or at least that's what they told him**

The world's most obsessive record collectors

Meet the men devoted to building the biggest vinyl archives in the world – and the DJs whose stacks of wax run into the hundreds of thousands.

Zero Freitas has taken record collecting to its logical conclusion. Not happy simply to have a sizeable number of records, the Brazilian businessman has made it his life's work to not only establish the biggest single collection anywhere in the world, but also to create a vast, listenable online archive of music.

Given that he estimates the size of his growing collection – housed in a warehouse in Sao Paulo – to be between six and eight million records, that's some task. To put that into context, Freitas owns roughly the same number of records as there are vinyl releases listed in the Discogs database. It's a staggering number of records in anybody's book.

According to articles in *The New York Times* and on the Vinyl Factory website, the Brazilian grew his awe-inspiring collection by stealth. Over the course of a decade, he put anonymous advertisements in newspapers and magazines around the world stating that he would pay more for whole collections than any other collector or record dealer. He acquired 200,000 records from a closed-down record shop in New York, 100,000 original Cuban records from a collector on the island, and even snapped up comedian Bob Hope's wax after he passed away.

The curious thing about Freitas is that he's not fussy about styles. While he naturally wants to own every vinyl record released in his native Brazil, he's also interested in records released in Africa, Asia and Europe. He apparently employs 'agents' around the world to hunt out sizeable private collections that he can gobble up. To Freitas, it's the volume that matters. He estimates that around 30% of his collection is 'duplicates' of records he already owns; eventually, these will be filtered out and sold.

↓ **Zero Freitas standing amidst the millions of records contained in his warehouse-sized archive in Sao Paulo, Brazil**
(Sebastian Liste, NOOR)

The first serious hoarder

Freitas's position as the world's greatest record collector is secure following his acquisition of the archive built up by Paul C. Mawhinney, former owner of the Record-Rama store in Pittsburgh, Pennsylvania. By the time the shop shut its doors in 2008, Mawhinney had built up a personal collection estimated to stand at well over three million items.

Mawhinney bought his first record in 1951, and by the time he established Record-Rama, his collection was already several thousand records deep. Throughout the store's lifespan, Mawhinney kept hold of at least one copy of every record he stocked.

By 1982, his collection was so large that he decided to catalogue it in a book called *MusicMaster*. Various volumes followed over the next decade, with original copies now worth more than many of the rare records

(Record-Rama)

listed in Mawhinney's exhaustive directories. Today, Mawhinney continues to catalogue vinyl releases via the Record-Rama Sound Archive Database, a searchable online database containing over half a million entries.

Nobody knows quite how much Zero Freitas paid for Mawhinney's collection, but it was once estimated to be worth an astonishing $50 million. Clearly, the Brazilian, whose family owns a public transport empire, has very deep pockets.

DJ's delight

There are very few people on Earth who can claim to own millions of records, but there are plenty who own tens or hundreds of thousands. In 2009, former BBC Radio 1 DJ Mike Read was forced to sell his collection of 120,000 7in singles and albums after filing for bankruptcy.

Read's collection, which was heavily weighted towards chart hits and popular music, was never quite as celebrated as that owned by his one-time Radio 1 colleague John Peel. When Peel passed away in 2004, his collection was said to include over 26,000 different albums, some 40,000 singles, and countless CDs.

← Long-serving DJ **Gilles Peterson's** record collection is so vast that he bought a house to store it in
(Casey Moore)

According to the John Peel Archive, a website that was established by the radio DJ's family after his death, the complete collection includes over 102,000 different items. Thrillingly, the Archive has pledged to catalogue all of these, placing them in an interactive online 'record shelf'. So far, around 2,700 of Peel's albums have been catalogued and added to the website's searchable database.

It makes sense that DJs like Peel and Mike Read would amass huge collections – after all, they not only used to make their living playing records to people, but were also given many thousands of free promotional records by artists and labels. The same rules apply for club DJs, and there are countless well-known selectors who have amassed epic collections.

Techno veteran Carl Cox, for example, claims to own at least 150,000 records, while legendary hip-hop producer Dr Dre once owned (but has now sold) a collection of 80,000 different singles and albums. Producer DJ Shadow, who built a career around making music out of samples lifted from obscure records, is estimated to own at least 60,000.

← Since he started DJing in his native Italy in the late 1970s, cosmic disco pioneer **Daniele Baldelli** has built up a collection of 65,000 records

When radio played vinyl

Before the days of CDs, streaming audio and digital music files, radio stations played records. Travel back with us to a time when vinyl made radio stations tick...

RIDING THE AIRWAVES WITH THE ORIGINAL PIRATE DJS

Up until 1973, the BBC had a monopoly on radio broadcasting in the UK. Since the corporation's 'public service' stations had to cater for a wide range of tastes, pop and rock-hungry listeners were often left wanting more. Their saviour came in 1964 with the launch of Radio Caroline, a pop service broadcast from a ship moored off the coast of Essex. The station was able to continue broadcasting from international waters thanks to a legal loophole.

Radio Caroline was a runaway success, and soon many other 'pirate radio' stations began broadcasting to the UK from positions offshore. While most of these were based on ships, a handful made their home in former Second World War forts originally erected to guard the entrance to the Thames Estuary.

The first to use one of these hulking metal structures was 'Screaming' Lord Sutch, later to find fame as the eccentric behind the Monster Raving Loony Party. He established Radio Sutch inside one of the five interconnected towers at Shivering Sands, before getting bored and handing the operation over to the founders of the Radio City pirate station. Nearby Roughs Tower became the base for Wonderful Radio in 1965, before being taken over by rival pirate radio DJ – and former army major – Paddy Roy Bates in 1967. He immediately renamed it The Principality of Sealand, abandoned his pirate radio ambitions and spent the rest of his life trying to get it recognised as a micronation.

← Radio Caroline achieved mythical status as an offshore challenger to the BBC (*Rob Olthof images: Hans Knot and offshoreradio.co.uk*)

The recording industry has not always had the best relationship with radio. When commercial radio stations began appearing in the United States in the 1920s, record companies tried to

prevent stations from broadcasting records on air. Musicians, too, were wary of the threat of recorded music, fearing that it would put them out of a job.

Of course, record companies' attitudes changed after the Second World War, when it soon became apparent that frequent radio play could help drive sales of singles and albums. Put simply, if a popular radio station or DJ played your record, it was more likely to become a hit. With so many records being released and only so many broadcasting hours in the day, airtime became a cherished commodity.

It wasn't long before record labels began setting up departments dedicated to radio promotion, staffed by 'pluggers', whose job it was to secure on-air coverage from DJs. Given the high stakes involved, it's perhaps unsurprising that some DJs in the United States were prosecuted for accepting money from pluggers to promote certain records (a practice dubbed 'payola').

Some radio DJs found fame by championing obscure records by new bands. British DJ John Peel (pictured) was a fixture on Radio 1 for the best part of 40 years. Throughout that time, he specialised in playing underground and alternative music, mostly off vinyl records that were sent to him by bands and small independent record labels.

Stacks of wax (and how to store it)

We've previously explained how to look after your records. Now it's time to discuss the different ways of storing them, including that inevitable trip to IKEA.

Gather two or more vinyl enthusiasts together and sooner or later the conversation will inevitably turn to record storage. Most collectors are rightly proud of their precious haul of vinyl and seemingly enjoy discussing the finer points of their shelving, boxes and filing system.

How you decide to store your records will partly depend on how many you have and the space at your disposal. There's no point committing to having floor-to-ceiling shelving custom built (and, believe us, plenty of people do) if you only have a few hundred records. Likewise, if you have thousands, a couple of milk crates or a selection of wooden boxes just won't do the job. There's also little more frustrating than buying a set of shelves and finding that they don't fit in the alcove you've singled out as a vinyl storage area.

Warp factor 9

Let's start with the basic rules of vinyl storage. First and foremost, records – whether in sleeves

↑ **Many record collectors choose to protect their fragile records and sleeves by popping them inside clear plastic 'oversleeves'. These are sleeves for LPs and 12in singles, but those for double albums, 7in and 10in singles are also available**

or outside of them – should never be stacked up on top of each other. Records are weighty things, and by stacking them you're adding a lot of pressure to those sat at the bottom of the pile. The vinyl may crack, scuff or warp.

When the disc is no longer perfectly flat, a record is said to be 'warped'. The distinctive bump around the record's perimeter that comes with warping can be caused by all manner of things but, more often than not, weight and/or heat is involved. That brings us neatly onto our second storage tip: never store your records in direct sunlight (so shelves should be placed away from windows), or adjacent to a heat source (eg hot water pipes or radiators).

Storage solutions

These days, there are so many different vinyl storage options, it can be hard to know where to begin. Those with relatively small record collections may find an all-in-one hi-fi unit, featuring space to store your amp, turntable and 50 to 100 records, an attractive proposition.

If you have more records than that but are still building up your collection, 'modular' storage systems could be the answer. A number of manufacturers now make stackable wooden 'crates' or boxes, or shelving for vinyl that can be expanded as your collection grows. For example, the Mapleshade Record Storage System is designed to lock together. Each shelf holds around 150 12in singles or albums, and you can easily add new shelves (space permitting) as your collection expands. Other modular shelving systems for records are also available, including some industrial-looking options from Cubitech.

For those with a sizeable collection, larger shelving units will be necessary. We like the look of the Boltz Record Storage Rack, a sturdy metal unit on wheels that can be pushed around the room. Each rack holds around 720 albums. If you require even more storage, then some of the major flat-pack furniture manufacturers, including the ubiquitous IKEA, sell shelving units that would fit the bill. Finally, if you're feeling really flush, why not ask a carpenter to build you some made-to-measure shelves? That way, you can make good use of whatever space you have available.

← If you plan to travel with records or begin a DJ career, you'll need to grab yourself a specially designed bag or box, such as this one

← Dovetail's range of record crates are made from solid oak or mahogany, making them more expensive than your average storage boxes

← IKEA's Kallax range of storage units are just the right size for albums, with an inch or two spare to make filing and arranging them that bit easier

Mining the past:
the rise of the record collector DJs

The DJ scene is changing, with the art of 'crate digging' now at the forefront for the first time in decades. We went to meet some of the dusty-fingered collectors currently making an impact on club culture to find out more.

Once, DJs competed with each other to acquire the hottest new white label promos – pre-release records slipped out in limited numbers for promotional purposes. These days, things are a little different.

Instead of fighting over the freshest records, many DJs are competing to find rare, obscure and expensive releases to put in their club sets and promotional mixes. If these happen to have previously been championed by DJs regarded as 'crate diggers' – the likes of DJ Harvey, Theo Parrish, Motor City Drum Ensemble or Young Marco, for example – so much the better.

Of course, dusty-fingered record collecting is not a new pursuit, and many DJ careers have been built on an ability to spot and secure lesser-known (or, for that matter, well known but impossible to find) gems.

Today, though, it seems more people are at it, and that those who excel at finding obscure

records are becoming celebrated scene heroes. Whereas DJs were once defined by their ability to read a dance floor, many are now judged purely on the rarity or financial worth of the records they play. It's certainly a turnaround of sorts.

Rare jazz and power showers

Zaf Chowdhry has seen it all over the last 30 years. Now co-owner of London's celebrated LoveVinyl store, Chowdhry has spent three decades buying and selling records. He's seen the record-collecting scene change a great deal over the last three decades, with dance floor trends – cyclical rises in interest in disco, boogie, soul, funk and Balearic beats – leading to a thriving crate-digging scene.

'Now, basically everybody's on it,' he laughs. 'I can't talk, because I'm in the business of doing reissues, but now it seems like everything is coming out again – even the really obscure

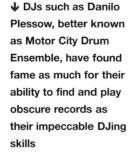
↓ DJs such as Danilo Plessow, better known as Motor City Drum Ensemble, have found fame as much for their ability to find and play obscure records as their impeccable DJing skills

stuff. It's a good thing, to be honest, because it highlights how much good music there is out there that never was discovered in the first place.'

Amongst collectors, Chowdhry is considered something of a 'don'. 'I remember I once went to Zaf's house, and within the first ten minutes I'd heard about £10,000 worth of records,' DJ and producer Ruf Dug says. 'He's just on another level.'

Chowdhry looks embarrassed when this story is relayed to him. 'I've started selling some nice stuff out of my jazz collection now,' he says. 'I'm getting to the age where I can sell five, six records, raise £500 or £600, and then buy a new shower, which I use every day. It's just a matter of priorities.'

Until the demands of running a business and parenthood took over, Chowdhry would frequently make trips abroad to hunt for wax – something that has always been considered a badge of honour for serious crate diggers. 'I've not been for about 15 years, but before that I used to head over to America once a year,' he says. 'There's nothing better than going somewhere and digging for yourself in obscure places. Each year it gets harder and harder, but people are still doing it.'

The rise in reissues of little-known music from Africa, in particular, has been driven by crate-digging tourists – DJs, collectors or record dealers willing to travel to the continent to find old warehouses full of surplus wax, lock-ups heaving with piles of forgotten gems and dusty shops that have seen better days.

This particular scene is notoriously competitive, with stories emerging of dealers willing to move to Nigeria or Ghana, for example, in order to make a living from 'flipping' records

(buying them cheap locally, in order to sell them on to collectors at vastly increased prices).

'It's a rat race – the competition and back stabbing is something else,' says Awesome Tapes From Africa founder Brian Shimkovitz. 'I don't want to sound like a snob, but I don't want to reissue any records that are listed on Discogs, that anybody else even knows about. It's funny that they're all fighting with each other, though.'

Shimkovitz's love of little-known African music is renowned, and originally went hand-in-hand with his academic interest in ethnomusicology (that's the study of the links between music and broader native culture).

'I know that people describe what I do as crate digging, but I don't see it as that, because I'm not specifically going to look for music,' he says. 'I'm going to various countries in Africa to visit and do research, and at some time during that month I'll be in shops, buying cassettes, or going to some person's old warehouse to see what they have left. I'm not one of these dudes who drops into a country, spends ten days digging, and then bounces.'

The Internet diggers

Predictably, the Internet is a thorny subject amongst some of the crate-digging DJs we spoke to. It's certainly true that the rise of Discogs Marketplace, in particular, has changed the record-collecting scene dramatically over the last decade.

Where once record collectors learnt of obscure, rare and expensive releases from other diggers or DJs, these can now be found with a few clicks online. Meanwhile, the rise in online DJ mix culture – and the MixesDB website, where vinyl nerds from around the world join

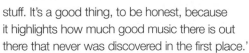

↖ Zaf Chowdhry behind the counter at LoveVinyl in London, the shop where he buys and sells rare and hard-to-find records

↑ Brian Shimkovitz has built a career out of finding and reissuing cassette-only albums, which he also uses in his DJ sets (Nick Yee/Hawaii Public Radio)

↑ **Manchester-based DJ/producer Ruf Dug revels in raiding bargain bins to find overlooked records for rock-bottom prices**

forces to identify unknown tunes in high-profile mix recordings – has made it easier for anyone with the time, money and inclination to build up a fantastic record collection without ever stepping foot in a record shop.

'For whatever reason, digging is cool, and playing old records is "the thing",' Ruf Dug says. 'Then it attracts other people as well. There are a heap of people who are into it and call themselves diggers, but they're just veracious YouTube heads.'

Ruf Dug is particularly critical of a certain strain of crate digging – and, it should also be noted, DJing – that equates a record's monetary value with its quality. 'All that Discogs does is give you market value for a particular record,' he says. 'It's a market, and it's a game. Sure, there are going to be some speculators, but that's just how capitalism works.'

Ruf Dug has, in part, built his DJ career on unearthing and championing records that others have overlooked. While admitting that the Internet is a great resource, he prefers to find odd and interesting records on the cheap – something that was once a backbone of both record collecting and DJ culture.

'I really do hold this belief that if something is more than a fiver, you're already too late,' he says. 'Someone already beat you to it, so what's the point? There are plenty more amazing 25p records that have yet to be played by DJ Harvey and be turned into a 50-quidder. I'd say the experience of finding great but overlooked records, for very little money, is a much more authentic experience than buying something celebrated and expensive online.'

Another 'digger' who subscribes to this mindset is Aiden D'Araujo, famed for his *House Hunting* column on the Ransom Note website. The regular feature celebrates D'Araujo's travels around London and beyond, seeking out cracking records for rock-bottom prices.

'I'll big up anyone who scores a house Holy Grail or wax want list weapon at a bargain price, but a lot of it is "look how much I've spent on this rare record", or "check out all the rare records in this mix",' he says. 'I know heads that will instantly disregard records on Discogs as the rating isn't nearly 5 out of 5, and they're under a fiver, so in their mind can't be good. They obviously haven't got a clue.'

He sighs. 'I feel the romance and ritual of record collecting is lost to the convenience of online ordering. A lot of heads just aren't patient any more – if they hear it, they've got to have it now.'

On the flipside, there are those within the scene who celebrate the way that the Internet has changed the game. Even Zaf Chowdhry, who co-manages a physical store and has long been a champion of the trusty old record shop, has good things to say about it.

'The Internet has changed everything,' he enthuses. 'I remember that pre-Internet, there came a time with disco and boogie that I thought I had it all. The Internet has just highlighted that there's ten or twenty times as much stuff out there than we previously thought, and my collection has got much bigger, just through the sharing of knowledge online.'

To enhance his argument further, Chowdhry highlights the experience of two twenty-something Norwegian friends of his, Frederick 'FredFades' Overlie and Hans-Jorgen 'DirtyHans' Waerner, who run the celebrated Touchdown parties in Oslo.

'Between them they have one of the best collections of private press 45s I've ever seen,' he enthuses. 'The shit they have is incredible. They've done it all through the Internet, hustling producers, being super nerds and being on it. There's no way that they'd have been able to do that without the Internet – it's just impossible.'

This ability to make connections with obscure artists and former record label owners online is something that has helped grow the offshoot archival release scene. It's that, and the immense detective work that goes with it, that we'll be focusing on next.

The record detectives

The rise of the reissue has been one of the trends helping to fuel the vinyl revival. Here we talk to some of the record collectors and label managers who spend their days trying to track down obscure artists in order to re-release their long forgotten music.

You can't fail to have noticed the sheer volume of vinyl reissues appearing in record stores of late. These vary wildly, from quirky 1980s new-wave pop, hard-to-find disco and boogie, forgotten ambient and eccentric new age grooves, to long out-of-print rock classics and previously unknown indigenous music from Africa, South America and the Middle East.

Amidst the record shop racks, you'll also find brilliantly researched compilations, artist retrospectives and first vinyl pressings of music that's been hidden on dusty master tapes for the best part of half a century. Our musical past is being successfully mined more than it has ever been before.

These days, it seems, obscurity sells; the rarer the original music, or the greater the story about how the reissue label came to find it, the more likely it is to find its way into the record collections of open-minded music buyers.

'The record buying public is a lot more knowledgeable now,' says Simon Purnell, co-founder of Leng Records and Spacetalk Records. 'They can find things on YouTube, and tap into their favourite DJs' record collections by listening to their mixes, and checking out their playlists. It's no coincidence that the shift towards people being more interested in obscure stuff began to happen when vinyl became more popular again.'

Hunting down the heads behind the heat

Purnell is one of a new breed of 'record detectives' – label managers or DJs who go to extreme lengths in order to track down artists and license their music. It's these people, and those they work closely with, who are behind the upsurge in officially licensed reissues and compilations.

'It's hard to get across how much work goes into licensing obscure music,' Purnell says. 'It's perceived as a pretty boring part of the process, because you're sat at a computer Googling for hours on end, trying to find people. When you find these people, the interesting part begins: learning about their lives, how they made the music, hearing their stories. It can sometimes take years of research and false starts to get to that point.'

⬇ Reissues and compilations of obscure old tracks often come with beautiful artwork and packaging, making them even more appealing to music fans and record collectors

The more obscure the music, the harder it can be to find people. When Brian Shimkovitz launched the *Awesome Tapes From Africa* blog in 2002, the first cassette he uploaded was Ata Kak's *Oba Simaa*. It took him almost a decade to find the little-known Ghanaian musician behind it, in order to license the album for re-release.

'I had no idea who he was, and none of my friends in Ghana had ever heard of him,' Shimkovitz says. 'There was no trace of him in the media, or among expat Ghanaians in Canada, where he had recorded the tape. When I eventually found him, it turned out he was a really cool guy – a very unique character. He only ever made this one tape, but now we've managed to book him live tours throughout the UK and Europe.'

Private investigations

Shimkovitz is full of these kinds of stories, but he's not alone. Stuart Leath, founder of the Emotional Rescue label that has delivered some of the most interesting reissues of recent years, is also happy to talk about his investigative methods.

'When I decided I wanted to reissue the Carl

& Carol Jacobs record ['Robot Jam'], I had no idea how to track them down,' Leath admits. 'Somehow I found out that Carl's band had been playing for 20 years at a restaurant in Florida. So I called the restaurant, and they said he'd gone back to Trinidad. Through some more work on the Internet I found a YouTube video filmed at his daughter's hairdressing salon, and Carl was in the video. I emailed the salon, asking if I could speak to him. Eight weeks later I got a reply, asking if I would call him. Sometimes it's easier than that, but it can also be a lot harder.'

Simon Purnell echoes Leath's sentiments. Since founding Leng Records with Paul 'Mudd' Murphy, he's worked extensively with Danny McLewin of DJ crew Psychemagik, on the outfit's acclaimed *Magik* series of crate-digging compilations. Along the way, he's spent countless hours chasing up leads, only for the trail to go cold.

'There have been a few times when I've had to be doggedly determined to find people,' he laughs. 'The Majik track on *Magik Sunset Part One*, "Take Me There", was the hardest one to license, because it was a self-released, private press thing, and there was pretty much no information on the original label. The writer credited said "McCormicork", which turned out to be an amalgamation of two people's names, one being the producer, Ray Cork Jr. I spent ages looking for a McCormicork, who of course didn't exist.'

The search didn't end there, though. Purnell decided to search through American White Pages phone book listings for leads, finding a Ray Cork Jr. in Los Angeles. Predictably, it was someone unrelated to the one-time producer and arranger he was looking for. Eventually, he narrowed down the search to a small town in Arizona.

'In a moment of inspiration, I decided to email the local Tourist Information Office to see if they'd heard of a guy called Ray Cork who used to be a music producer,' he remembers. 'A few days later I got a reply saying they'd forwarded my email onto him. A couple of days after that Ray emailed me, saying, "You've found me, what do you want?"'

Purnell bursts into laughter at the memory, before recalling how the story progressed

⬇ Before finding fame as a DJ and producer, Psychemagik's Danny McLewin spent years working as a record dealer specialising in rare vinyl *(PRS For Music)*

after that. 'Once I started talking to him, I sent him some information about the project and offered him an advance against royalties. He replied asking for even more information, because his wife thought it was an Internet scam! You can completely understand it, though. It probably did look a little strange.'

Cork agreed to the license request, McLewin re-edited the track, and it became one of the most popular cuts on the *Magik Sunset Part One* compilation. Of course, not all licence requests go this well: some artists, especially those whose short-lived music careers ended decades ago, are not so receptive.

'I would say that for every reissue I put out, there are ten where I've tried and failed,' Stuart Leath says. 'That can be because I can't find the artist, they're not interested, or another reissue label has got there first.'

Just as record collecting is a notoriously competitive business, so is the reissue industry. Stuart Leath and Brian Shimkovitz have both received online abuse from people involved in other reissue labels. 'I have no ego about it,' Leath says. 'If another label gets there first, then fair enough. At the end of the day, it's about the original artist and the record itself, not the specific label that reissues it.'

For all the competiveness and the sheer hard work it can take to track down artists in order to license tracks or releases, all of those we spoke to said it could be hugely rewarding. 'There's a story in every record,' says leading LoveVinyl co-founder Zaf Chowdhry. 'People move on, do different things in their lives and forget that they made some of these records. In order to reissue Martin L. Dumas' "Attitude & Belief", I tracked down his widow and children. They were elated that somebody wanted to put out his music again. The fact that it was unexpected probably made it more exciting for them. It's a good thing.'

There are numerous examples of previously obscure artists whose careers have been re-ignited by contemporary reissues of their work. Previously little-known ambient producer Gigi Masin has become a man in demand following Music From Memory's 2013 retrospective of his work, while a number of the artists championed by *Awesome Tapes*

From Africa have returned to live performance after years away.

'In some cases it's a really life-changing thing,' Brian Shimkovitz says. 'Hailu Mergia from Ethiopia had been driving a taxi in Washington DC for 30 years, and until we re-released his album, he'd not performed for 25 years. Now he's out there doing it again, though he still does drive his cab!'

Not all reissue labels develop relationships with the artists whose music they rerelease, but those that do make the effort can sometimes be rewarded. The first release on Danny McLewin, Simon Purnell and Paul Murphy's Spacetalk Records imprint was a reissue of a ridiculously obscure, private press record from a 1970s duo called Morrison Kincannon. Once Purnell had done a deal with Norman Morrison to re-release the record, the Californian – now an estate agent – began sending him large amounts of unreleased music, all of which was recorded during the same period.

'I think we're up to 60-plus tracks now,' Purnell reveals. 'We asked him to send them all over so we could put together an album. It's a good example of nurturing a relationship with an artist through mutual respect – he feels happy doing this project with us.'

↑ Almost two years after Simon Purnell tracked down Norman Morrison, Spacetalk Records released *Morrison Kincannon*, an album full of 1970s recordings that had previously sat dormant on reel-to-reel tapes for nearly 40 years

The joy of vinyl

What is it about 'wax' that's so addictive? We asked a host of well-known record collectors to tell us what it is about vinyl that turns them on.

Keb Darge ↓

Scottish DJ and record producer

In about 1983 I went through a warehouse with about 70,000 mainly Sixties 45s in it. I turned up the next weekend to do my set at the Stafford all-nighter with a box full of killer new discoveries. Records nobody had ever heard of before. It blew the roof off the place and even brought the undead from the record bar out of their shadows, and onto the dance floor. The venues back then had a room or large space at the back for a number of record dealers to ply their trade in. The stage got swamped with serious collectors all wanting a glance at these new future anthems. Being the nasty man that I am though, I had covered up most of the labels.

Bill Brewster →

Journalist and author of *Last Night A DJ Saved My Life*

I am not a completist. I do not collect first editions. I love CDs (and tapes and minidisks and WAVs and MP3s). I've never spent more than £150 on a record. I get more pleasure finding hidden gems for a quid than chasing

big-ticket items. But I am, unquestionably, addicted to the pursuit of music. I have a small room in my house which houses all of my music and it's like a calm but chaotic sanctuary where no-one else goes and is not welcome (unless they are also a record fiend). When I need some private time, I go there. It's like a potting shed for records. It's not about money or worth. They are my memories. Most of the records I truly love and would rescue from a fire are utterly worthless to anyone but me. But they're the ones I cherish. I pity anyone who values an eBay price over a beautiful piece of music.

DJ Jazzy Jeff →

Hip hop and R & B DJ, actor, comedian
I fought the 45 addiction for a long time because I knew exactly what would happen if I jumped back in. And it did. Someone handed me the phones at a mixing competition and it wafted me back in time. Those 45s have become really big again because people appreciate the static and the texture. I've got records in my front room, in my basement, in my garage, in my mom's house, in storage –

(Paul Duffy)

maybe 50,000 or 60,000 records, although that's a super-guess and like all real vinyl collectors I don't organise it properly. It's like a scavenger hunt in my own house when I try to find anything.

Andy Smith ↑

DJ from East London

I am one of the few DJs that still carries bags of 7in singles to clubs around the world. I toured the world with the band Portishead in the late 90s and bought records wherever the band played. The best ever trawl was in New Orleans where the 7in singles were 20c each. The shop was only open for another half hour and I literally got bags and just threw anything in that was on an interesting label, passing them to the guy at the store to add up whilst moving onto the next bag. I got backstage to the gig and listened to hundreds of unknown tracks, just taking the good ones. There may well still be a pile of unwanted records backstage at the 'House of Blues' in New Orleans to this day.

Gilles Peterson

French DJ and record label owner

My vinyl is spread over three properties and I don't actually know exactly where everything is. I like a bit of chaos, because it allows me to come across stuff unexpectedly and go off in new directions. I don't know the exact number of records in my collection, but it's probably about 70,000, amassed over 35 years. The craziest is *The Planet Is Alive… Let It Live!* by Sarah Vaughan. The car brand Alfa Romeo paid for it to be produced for Pope John Paul II, whose poems were the basis for some of the lyrics. You couldn't make it up.

Pezz

Owner, 3 Beat Records, Liverpool

It all started for me back in '79 at the age of 11. Armed with my pocket money, off I went to the record shop to buy Gary Numan 'Cars' on 7". Once I'd overcome the trepidation of going in and buying this first one and getting it home to play, I was instantly hooked. Forty thousand records later I still can't stop. Early days it was pop electronica, then electro, hip hop and soul. House music then took over, which led me to running 3 Beat Records for 18 years. My obsession with those wonderful round black discs has never faded and never ever will....

DJ Spinna ↓

American hip hop producer from Brooklyn

My vinyl collection represents a lifetime of personal experiences. I've been buying records since I was nine years old and haven't stopped since. It's more than an addiction... at this point it's a lifestyle. I plan my entire life (from buying groceries and paying bills) around records. I think it's one of the most diverse collections on the planet. If you comb through it, you will find progressive rock, deep spiritual jazz, blues, deep funk, northern soul, Brazilian, techno, house, new age, experimental, European soundtracks, Caribbean, children's records, comedy, disco, R&B, hip hop, punk, weird oddballs and even vintage jazz 78s from the '40s and '50s, and more. I'm constantly learning from my own collection while simultaneously curating it by weeding out useless promos and free records I've accumulated over time. I want to get to that point where every record you pull is an absolute gem. Yet, I still feel incomplete. There's still so much I need and I'm always on the hunt for new discoveries or obscure titles. Just when you think you know it all, the universe surprises you with something crazy. The journey never ends.

(V Shootz)

Former world snooker no. 1 and DJ

It first hit me in my teens. After *Tubular Bells*, Virgin produced a couple of albums sold at a loss to get people interested in prog rock, one by Faust called *Faust* and one by Gong called *Camembert Electrique*. They were 57p or 59p I think. Back then I was a fan of the game of chess and a fan of prog rock, both dirty words and synonymous with boring people. But I was a child of the prog rock era: if you possessed an Afghan coat you were required to be into it. Now it's quite hip and there's even a magazine in WH Smith on prog rock.

There's definitely an addiction element to collecting records – you just feel you need to own it. It's almost like the record chooses you and you don't have any choice in the matter. There's a massive difference between the physical of a piece of vinyl and the ones and noughts of digital.

I've tried to keep my collection all in one place and have about 8,000 soul singles and 5,000 albums, which is nothing really. The singles are all catalogued, but the albums are grouped, would you believe, by country because of the different music scenes of, say, Germany or France. It includes 'Canterbury', which admittedly is not a country, after the prog rock Canterbury Sound.

There was a time in the 1990s when I bought and sold records with a mate who produced a fanzine called *Voices From The Shadows*. It was about the weird world of soul singles, which is a rabbit hole within a rabbit hole.

The most I've ever paid for a single is about £400 and upsettingly I remember selling one on eBay for £200, something dancey and modern, and I saw it a short time later on sale for $6,000. Mind you, I bought 1,600 soul singles in one go for £800 and sold three for £800, meaning I had 1,597 free records left.

I still buy records and do a radio show on a local community radio station, so it's my responsibility to keep buying stuff by new acts.

(Yuko Asanuma)

Colleen 'Cosmo' Murphy

DJ and founder of Classic Album Sundays

When I was 12 years old, two important things happened: my dad gave me a hand-me-down GE Trimline record player and my uncle Dennis let me loose on his record collection. Dennis was on the right side of 30 and pretty cool. He had stuff from the Beatles, the Stones and Crosby Stills & Nash, but one record with a gloriously cosmic album cover sticks in my memory, *Days of Future Passed* by The Moody Blues. That was the beginning of my obsession with vinyl and the album format.

When I was 14 I had my own vinyl-only radio show on my high school's 10-watt radio station, and at 16 I worked at a record shop after school, where I spent part of my wages, along with other cool spots like Planet, Nuggets, Newbury Comics and Loony Tunes in Boston. After working in college radio I became a regular at David Mancuso's Loft, was inspired to start collecting old soul and disco and bought two Technics 1200s (which I still have) and a CMA 10-2DL Bozak – the best mixer ever and lovingly reconditioned.

My record collection has been culled through several moves and as I believe it is not about quantity but quality, I should have about 20,000 records but instead have kept an amazing 10,000 in my record library (one of my favourite places in the world). My collection is organised by genre and some of the sections are even alphabetised, but the most important thing is I can find everything. And when I flick through the shelves, these records tell the story of my life.

My obsession with vinyl has found its culmination with my Classic Album Sundays venture, which taps into the way we listen to music in the 21st century and the album format. Vinyl isn't just about the music but it's about the overall experience – the transcendental sound of a great pressing, the life energy, the artwork, the tactility, the scent, the sense of engagement and the ritual. I'm writing this in Japan after three seven-hour vinyl DJ sets on consecutive nights (and very little sleep), but I know the next time I put something on the turntable my energy will come flooding back.

Chapter Five

Vinyl technique

DJing for beginners

Fancy putting your record collection to good use? If so, DJing could be for you. Whether you collect jazz, rock, reggae, house or disco, there's nothing quite like playing your favourite music to people in public.

↓ For every high-profile DJ entertaining crowds of thousands in superclubs and at music festivals, there are thousands of others who just mix at home for fun

There was a time when DJing was the sole preserve of scarily obsessive record collectors, excitable party animals and those who enjoyed playing very bad music at weddings. In those days, the ability to pick up a microphone and announce the arrival of a taxi was as integral to the DJ's job as selecting and sequencing songs.

DJ culture has certainly come on a lot since then. Today, leading DJs are as much part of the entertainment industry as musicians, actors and television personalities. For those who reach the commercial summit, the financial rewards are impressive. DJs operating in that top tier can earn as much in a weekend as some people make in an entire year.

They are, though, the exception to the rule. For every sunglasses-clad 'superstar DJ' jumping around on stage in front of 10,000 people, there are a hundred more plying their trade in local bars and clubs for little or no money. There are even more whose DJing ambitions stretch no further than mixing music at home, showcasing their record collection on Internet radio shows and occasionally dropping a few little-known gems at a friend's house party.

Your average DJ is not a multi-millionaire jetting around the world to play at music festivals, but rather a dedicated record collector with a desire to share music they love with other people. Doing this in public appeals to most DJs, but mixing itself – the art of selecting, sequencing and blending music into a coherent and entertaining set of songs – is an enjoyable pastime in its own right.

Style and substance

Some dedicated DJs, especially those who've been doing it a long time, can be understandably protective about their chosen pursuit. They rightly see it as a valid musical art form and consider the best DJs to be masters of their craft. These are men and women who have spent years or decades not only honing their technical skills, but also developing a distinctive personal style.

Just as guitarists, drummers and pianists can be identified by their playing style, great DJs have a distinctive way of selecting, sequencing and mixing records that sets them apart. Think of the all-action quick mixing of techno legend Jeff Mills, the turntable trickery of hip-hop greats such as Grandmaster Flash and Grand Wizzard Theodore or the long, melodic blends preferred by progressive house mainstays such as Sasha and John Digweed.

As much as these artists, and many others, have elevated DJing to a whole new level, it doesn't have to be this complicated. The fundamental basics of DJing are actually relatively simple to learn and even more advanced techniques can be perfected through practice. Put simply: anyone can be a DJ.

I am the DJ

The most important thing you need to be a DJ is a passion for music. Since you're reading

↑ **Many DJs showcase their record collections via sets at local bars and pubs. You can find out how you can do the same later in this chapter**

this book, we can assume that you fall into that category. Whether you own 50 records or 50,000, the very fact that you're a vinyl enthusiast makes you perfect DJ material. After all, the vast majority of vinyl DJs started out as record collectors.

It doesn't particularly matter what style of music you're passionate about playing, either. While many DJs specialise in playing music that people dance to – be it classic soul, 1970s disco, acid house, contemporary EDM or drum & bass – there are plenty of others with little or no interest in club culture. Whether you're a rock fan, jazz enthusiast or indie kid, you have just as much right as anyone else to become a DJ. Secure yourself a pair of DJ-friendly turntables and a mixer, and you'll be ready to start your DJing adventure.

Mixing basics

The first step on your DJing journey is to master the fundamental skill of 'mixing' records together. Here's our quick-start guide for beginners...

For now, we're going to assume that you already own a very basic vinyl DJing set-up of two turntables – either belt-drive, or direct-drive, with pitch control – and a mixer. To mix, you'll also need a sturdy pair of headphones that can be plugged into the mixer and a pair of slipmats. DJs use these instead of the solid rubber mats that normally ship with turntables. Like their rubber counterparts, slipmats are placed between the metal platter and the record you want to listen to (or, in this case, mix with).

If you've just acquired DJing equipment, it's a good idea to spend a little time getting accustomed to the various features. In the case of the turntables, that means things like the stop/start button and, more importantly, the pitch control used to adjust the speed at which the platter spins.

When it comes to the mixer, there are a few more controls to get to grips with before learning to mix. Pay close attention to the

channel faders and channel EQs. These are used to alter the volume and sound dynamics of the music being played on each turntable. In most instances, these will be accompanied by a crossfader, which sits below the channel faders. Moving the crossfader from right to left (or vice-versa) allows you to select which record comes out of the mixer into your amplifier. Stick it in the central position and you'll hear a blend of both tracks – providing the channel faders are pushed up, of course.

Every DJ mixer also comes with headphone monitoring controls. The layout of these varies depending on the make and model, but all offer the opportunity to listen to one or both channels, even when the mixer's master volume is turned down. This enables DJs to find and select the appropriate part on the record before mixing it in. To allow easier 'monitoring' of a mix, most DJ mixers boast a control knob or slider that allows you to listen to a blend of the record you want to mix in and the one currently playing on the other turntable (usually the 'master' output).

Once you're comfortable with the various controls and what they do, you're ready to learn the fundamentals of DJing technique.

Hands-on control

In some ways, DJing is counter-intuitive. In general, touching vinyl records is a no-no. Sticking your fingers on the surface of a record leads to grubby fingerprints and, over time, a reduction in sound quality. If you're fussy about these things – and, let's face it, most record collectors are – then you should think twice about DJing. While it is possible to do basic mixes without manhandling your precious wax, you're not going to get very far as a DJ. It's a

hands-on art form and the sooner you get used to that idea, the better.

So how should you handle records while they're on the decks? With your fingertips, that's how. Put a record on the left turntable, place the needle on the surface and press the stop/start button to get the platter spinning. As the first song kicks in, quickly place your fingertips on the surface of the record to stop the record and hold it in place. If you've caught it correctly, the turntable platter should continue to spin beneath the static record.

While still holding the record, pull it towards you slightly. You'll hear the music slowly playing backwards. When you reach the exact start point of the song, hold it in place again. When you're ready to let the record play, raise your fingers to 'drop' the track. This process of stopping, starting and manipulating records by hand while they're on a turntable is known as 'slip-cueing'.

Your first mix

You should now have a song playing on the left turntable. Now have a look at your DJ mixer. Is the crossfader set to the channel that the left deck is plugged into, with the channel fader pushed up? If so, you should be hearing the song through your speakers. When this song ends, you're going to perform your first mix.

Whack a record on the right turntable but don't set it spinning just yet. Instead, turn your attention to the mixer. Is the channel fader

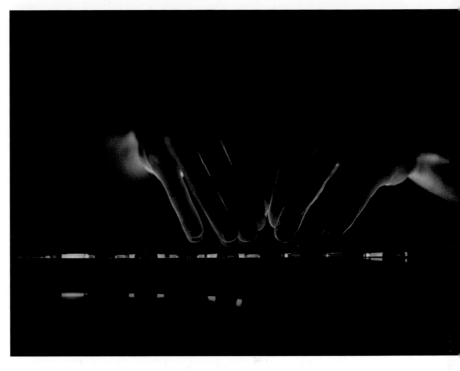

relating to that deck pushed up? If so, pull it right down. You're now going to do some slip-cueing on the right deck, but this time you're going to monitor the sound in the headphones.

To do this, you'll need to make sure the mixer's monitoring controls are set to 'cue' or 'pre-fade listen' on that channel. Once you've done that, start playing the record and stop it with the fingers of your right hand using the method described above. Push or pull the record to find the start point of the song and then hold it in place as the platter spins below.

As the song playing on the left turntable gets into its final stages, push up the fader of the channel the right turntable is connected to. Both faders should now be pushed up, or 'open'. Remember that you should still be holding the record in place with your fingertips.

As the song playing on the left deck begins to fade out, start dragging the mixer's crossfader from left to right and lift the fingers of your right hand to start the record playing. To complete the mix, pull down the original fader so all that you can now hear through the speakers is the record playing on the right turntable. You've now completed your first mix!

Practice makes perfect

The methods and movements involved with DJing can feel awkward at first, but will soon become second nature. Spend a few hours slip-cueing and mixing records together and you'll soon be comfortable with it.

Once you've perfected slip-cueing with both hands, you can try getting a little more advanced. When releasing the record to 'drop it' into the mix, give it a little push as you release your fingers. You're not looking for a weighty shove, but rather a nudge that's forceful enough to get the record going until the turntable platter takes over.

TEACH YOUR SON OR DAUGHTER TO MIX

There's something about a DJ set-up of two turntables and a mixer that captures the imagination of children. If you have kids, sooner or later they'll take an interest in your decks. If they do, try teaching them to mix in an even more basic way than the method already described.

Set the mixer's crossfader to the central position. Ask your son or daughter to place a record on the left turntable and carefully place the needle down at the start of the first track. Tell them to push the applicable channel fader up and press the stop/start button to play the song. Next, get them to place a record on the right turntable and select a track to play.

When the first song is about to end, tell them to push up the spare channel fader so both are now open. At the right moment, ask them to press the start button on the right turntable.

As the first record speeds towards its conclusion, tell your son or daughter to push up the second channel fader and press 'start' on the right deck. Finally, ask them to pull down the first channel fader and complete their first mix.

The beat goes on

Most people associate DJing with the ability to mix records together in time, so that the drumbeats never stop. This technique is known as 'beat matching', and it has been the backbone of club DJing since the early 1980s.

Beat matching is not the easiest thing for beginners to learn. While you can grasp the fundamental concept and method quite quickly, perfecting it can take weeks, months or even years of practice. Get the right two records in time for long enough, though, and you may find the mythical 'third track' – a unique blend of two songs that sounds superb in its own right.

Time and tempo

To beat match, you need to get the drums of two different songs in time with each other long enough to perform a smooth mix. This can be done using the pitch adjustment control fader

↓ Many of the most celebrated club DJs of all time can not only 'beat match', but also keep the drums of two records in time for extended periods

found on DJ-friendly turntables. Push the pitch control fader away from your body to slow down the turntable platter; pull it towards you to speed it up.

When it comes to DJing, the tempo of music is measured in 'beats per minute', or 'BPM' for short. The vast majority of house and disco records tend to have a tempo of between 115 and 125 beats per minute. Techno tends to be faster – around the 130 to 140 BPM range – while drum & bass is even speedier, often up around 160–180 BPM.

It is possible to work out the tempo of a track, in beats per minute, yourself. Simply put on a record and count the number of beats you hear in 15 seconds. Multiply this number by four, and you've found your BPM. So, if you count 30 beats in 15 seconds, the song's BPM is 120. If you'd rather not perform any mental arithmetic, numerous BPM counter applications are available for smartphones.

Match those beats

When you're ready to try your first beat matched mix, select two records with a similar BPM tempo and put them on the decks. If you own DJ-friendly dance records with sections of 'open beats' at the beginning and end, use those – it's a lot easier to match the drums if you don't have to worry about basslines, piano stabs or guitar licks.

Start the first record playing, set the mixer's crossfader to the central position and push up the correct channel fader. Sound should now be coming through your speakers. If the second channel fader is up, pull it down to zero.

Use the headphones to locate the first beat of the record on the other turntable. Adjust the headphone monitoring controls so you can hear a mixture of the track currently playing, and the one you're about to mix in. Start the track on the second turntable playing by 'dropping' it into the mix. Ideally, you should try and 'catch' the

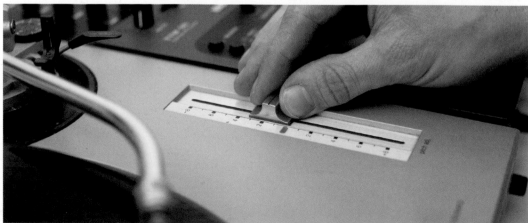

kick-drum of the first record, so both beats sound in time.

Let both records play and listen carefully in your headphones. Is the record you're about to mix in playing faster or slower than the other one? If it's slower, the beats will sound like they're 'lagging behind' those on the first record. Conversely, if it's faster, you'll hear the beats of the second record slightly ahead of those on the first.

Try to get the drumbeats of the two records as synchronised as possible. You can subtly adjust the speed of either record using the applicable turntable's pitch control function. Be careful with the pitch fader: big movements in either direction will speed up or slow down the record dramatically, potentially ruining your chances of nailing the mix.

If you think you're ready to attempt a beat matched mix, cue-up the record on the second turntable again and hold it in place with your fingers. As the first record gets into its closing stages, drop the second record. If you've successfully caught the beat, they should be in time. If they are, bring up the second channel fader on the mixer so that the sounds of both records are coming out of the speakers. Finally, pull down the first channel fader to complete the mix.

GET YOUR OWN DJ TUTOR

If you're serious about becoming a DJ and want to speed up the learning process, you might find tuition useful. Many experienced DJs now earn a living, in part at least, by offering one-on-one training. They will demonstrate key techniques, offer tips for improving your mixes and even show you a few tricks of the trade.

Some offer intensive crash courses, while others will allow you to learn through weekly sessions of a couple of hours. Experienced tutors, like great teachers, will be patient when you make mistakes and offer encouragement. After all, they were once rookie DJs, too. If your budget won't stretch to employing a tutor, you can also find plenty of instruction videos online.

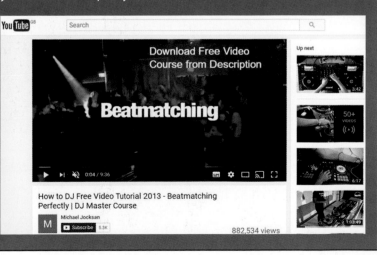

Advanced techniques

Once you've got the hang of mixing and beat matching, you may have had your fill of DJ practice. If not, there are plenty more advanced techniques and tricks to learn.

In this section, we're going to focus on DJing techniques that take a little more time to master. Most are relatively straightforward and some experienced DJs may think of them as essential skills, rather than hugely advanced tricks. All, though, are a step up from the basic mixing techniques previously outlined in this chapter.

Some of these tricks will help you keep two tracks in the mix for longer in order to create more impressive blends of music, while others can be used to add colour and drama to your sets. Practised enough, all will make you a far more skilful DJ.

↓ Scratch DJs, sometimes known as turntablists, use their turntables and mixer to perform impressive tricks such as beat-juggling, which involves quickly mixing between two copies of the same record to change the drum patterns the audience hears, a technique pioneered by the legendary Grandmaster Flash *(Andy Sheppard/Redferns via Getty Images)*

Better beat matching

Some DJs prefer short beat matched mixes, while others like to extend their mixes by keeping two songs in time for a longer period. Experienced DJs can do this by 'riding the pitch' on one or more decks, making subtle adjustments using the pitch control fader during the mix. You can also use your fingers to manhandle different parts of the turntable platter to subtly speed up or slow down a record during playback.

To slow down a record while in the mix, gently run the tips of your middle finger and forefinger down the sloping edge of the rotating turntable platter. You'll need a deft touch, though – if you touch the platter's edge too heavily, the record will slow down so much that you run the risk of ruining the mix completely.

If a record you're mixing in is starting to lag behind the other one, you can get things back on track by grabbing the turntable's centre spindle between thumb and forefinger and giving it a quick 'tweak'. What you're trying to do is momentarily make the platter rotate quicker in order to make the record 'catch up' with the one you're mixing into.

Alternatively, you can manually push the record round by placing your forefinger and middle finger (or just one of those) on the centre label. Again, a deft touch is needed to avoid any dramatic speeding up (and the woozy noise that goes with it).

Turntablist techniques

Turntablism is the art of using the decks and mixer to perform amazing routines that combine a number of different high-level DJ techniques. It's been a big part of hip-hop culture since the mid-1970s, when Grandmaster Flash developed a technique to seamlessly extend short passages of drumbeats using two copies of the same record.

Today, top turntablists perform a range of hard-to-master techniques with such fancy names as 'transformer', 'flare' and 'chirp'. These are all different 'scratches' – sounds made by manually manipulating a record and, in some cases, quick crossfader movements.

You'll find instruction videos on all of these scratches, and more, online. Here, we're going

to concentrate on two simpler techniques: the baby scratch and the Scribble scratch.

The baby scratch

To perform a baby scratch, find a 'clean' sound to manipulate, such as the first kick-drum of a dance record. Cue it up and hold it in place with your fingers. When you want to perform the scratch, push the record forward so that the sound plays, and then pull it back into the starting position. While some of the movement required to perform the baby scratch comes

from the wrist, it's your knuckles and fingers that should be doing most of the work.

The Scribble scratch

The Scribble is a more refined version of the baby scratch, performed with the arm held straighter and higher, and the fingers closer together. You're aiming to make smaller, quicker movements backwards and forwards to get a shorter scratching sound. Compared to the baby scratch, your wrist and arm should be more rigid, with the quick and slight movement coming from the elbow.

WHAT'S THAT NOISE?

Hip-hop DJ, producer and actor Jazzy Jeff fell in love with records at an early age. It wasn't long before he became obsessed with the alien sound of 'scratching'. He said: 'I owe my love of vinyl to my brothers who would go out to work and let me play their records when I was six or seven years old. They taught me how to look after records and later on I studied the way each track was produced to understand how the sound had been created. I learnt how to scratch on my mom's dining room table. I didn't want her to say, "What's that noise?", so I tried really hard to make the scratching part of the sound, rather than just noise. I tried to make it as appealing as possible, a complement to the music.'

The art of the DJ

There's more to DJing that having competent technical skills. If you want to be the best, you need to hone your craft, just as any top tradesman or woman would...

While DJing technique is naturally important, the only people who really care if your mixes are a little rough round the edges are other DJs. They can be a judgemental lot at times, but tend to be more critical of their own performance than those of fellow 'jocks'. It's why you'll find them purring over the sets of top-quality DJs – those who combine high technical skills with individual style and the ability to adapt to the needs of their audience.

Developing your own style and learning to tailor sets to specific crowds takes time and experience. Nobody expects novice DJs to get it right first time, but you can give yourself a greater chance of success if you take the following advice on board.

Prepare properly

If you're going to play a set in public – be it in a club, bar or even to a group of friends – make sure you've given it some thought beforehand. If you're packing a bag of records, don't just sling 50 slabs of wax into a bag and hope for the best. Think about tailoring the records you pack to the type of set you're being asked to do. For example, if you're playing in the mid-afternoon at a barbecue, it probably isn't appropriate to turn up with three hours of heavy techno. Likewise,

↓ Some high-profile DJs, such as Harvey, are widely considered to be masters of their art, with an ability to work a dance floor through a combination of programming and understanding the desires of dancers *(Natt Lim/Getty Images for FYF)*

if you've been asked to drop a few tunes at a birthday party, you'll almost certainly get a better response if you play recognisable, well-known songs rather than obscure underground dubstep cuts (unless, of course, that's what your host has asked for).

Learn about 'warm-up' and 'peak-time'

If you're going to be DJing in a club, find out what time you'll be on, and who is playing after you, before packing your records. By and large, most club nights can be divided into two portions.

First is the warm-up, when the DJ sets the tone for the evening and gently draws people onto the dance floor. Think warm, groovy and ear-pleasing: the kind of music that will get you off your seat, but doesn't take too much energy to dance to.

The second portion of the night is known as peak-time. This is when the dance floor is at its busiest and the dancers still have energy to burn. Peak-time DJs are there to make sure everyone has a great time and goes home happy. They can usually get away with quite a lot, especially at venues with an underground music policy, but have to be prepared to sling on the odd anthem now and then to give the crowd a lift.

↓ **Peak-time audiences are gagging to go wild at the DJ's selections. It's your job to give them what they want – or, more accurately, what you think they'll respond positively to**

Try to read the dance floor

This is where DJing becomes a genuine art form. Experienced DJs can study the crowd of dancers they have in front of them, and adjust their sets accordingly to solicit the best response. For example, they might notice that the assembled dancers respond well to records they don't know, or conversely that they'll only keep dancing if they hear songs they can sing along to.

Similarly, great DJs might play heavier records if they judge that the dance floor needs an injection of energy, or go a bit deeper and groovier if dancers look like they're flagging. As the exact make-up of a crowd can change over the course of an evening, DJs need to be reading the dance floor throughout their set. Smart DJs will also spend time studying the dancers before they play, too; after all, you can learn a lot from what other DJs do right and wrong.

Do-it-yourself!

Gigs can be hard to come by for new DJs. That's why more and more people are putting on their own intimate events in local pubs, bars and community centres. Here's how you could do the same, too…

Now you've learned some of the skills you'll need to become a rock-solid DJ, it's about time you tested them out on the general public. If those words fill you with dread, don't worry: it's a big step and it's only natural to be a little apprehensive. What you're forgetting, though, is that DJing is about more than making rooms full of excitable youngsters dance like mad to throbbing underground dance music.

First and foremost, you can DJ with any kind of music you can think of, regardless of whether it has been designed to make people dance or not. For example, it's not uncommon to walk into a suburban pub on a Sunday afternoon and find someone spinning dusty old jazz records. Similarly, there are plenty of DJs who play regular sets of classic rock, energy-packed punk and '80s pop. If you want to play laid-back folk records, storming Polish disco singles or 1950s rock 'n' roll seven-inches, you can. Fundamentally, there are no rules.

Be proactive

If you want to play music to people, be proactive. It is possible to secure slots at existing events by chatting to those who run them, though your lack of previous experience may be held against you. If you want to take this approach, the best option is to talk to any friends who DJ in public. They may be willing to let you play a few records at one of their nights, or at the very least introduce you to venue managers and event promoters.

Our advice, though, is to do it yourself and put on a small 'night' of your own. This way you have total control: you can decide what kinds of records are played, come up with a name that fits the sort of music you'll be playing and even choose who else plays alongside you.

You might think this is a big task, but it's actually really easy. Don't think too big to begin with. Instead of approaching clubs, talk to pub landlords and bar managers. They may have a function room that can be hired out for events at a small cost (which is sometimes refunded if they take a certain amount of money in drinks sales), or be open to DJs playing in the pub or bar at weekends. If you don't ask, you'll never know!

It goes without saying that you should approach venues you think may suit the kinds of music you want to play. For example, a pub with a slightly older clientele might not be too keen on 20-year-olds banging out super-fast trance records, but they may be open to the idea of middle-aged men and women dropping psychedelic rock, Jamaican dub or '80s jazz-funk. Similarly, student bar managers might be open to contemporary dance music, but turn their nose up at progressive rock or classic jazz.

⬇ **Some of the most enjoyable DJ sets are those played in relaxed, intimate surroundings, where there's no pressure to satisfy the demands of a dance floor**

Recording your own mix

If you've got some favourite tracks and a few hours to spare, it's easier than you think to create a mix. Start printing the promotional flyers now...

Those of a certain age will have fond memories of exchanging 'mix tapes' – homemade compilations of favourite songs, gathered together on a badly labelled C60 or C90 cassette. The ability to create a killer mix tape, either by recording individual tracks off records or snatching them from radio broadcasts, was a skill that could lift your social standing by several notches – at least among fellow music nerds.

Given that DJs are, by and large, massive music geeks, it's perhaps unsurprising that they've embraced mix-tape culture. While the format may have changed – these days downloadable MP3 files of mixes are far more popular than cassettes or CDs – the desire to record and share mixes is still inside every DJ's DNA.

There are very good reasons that DJs record mixes. For starters, it's a way of showing off your record collection and proving to listeners – particularly other DJs – that you have impeccable music taste. If you own rather a lot of obscure, sought-after records, sticking them on a seamlessly blended and beat matched mix will enhance your reputation as a crate digger and selector.

For DJs, mix recordings are the next best thing to a CV bulging with the names of hyped clubs and festivals they've played at. Effectively, it's the DJ's chance to show off: the audio equivalent of whipping your shirt off to reveal bulging biceps and a finely sculpted 'six-pack'. Since most DJs don't have a resume that boasts appearances at

→ **John Digweed regularly releases epic DJ mixes, which sometimes run to five or six CDs in length**
(Daniel Zuchnik via Getty)

top 'destination' clubs – or a six-pack, for that matter – recording killer mixes is their best chance to attract the attention of club promoters and venue managers.

Anyway you wanna

There's no set formula for a recorded DJ mix. Some people use their mixes as a showcase for what they could do in a club environment, while others concentrate on creating something that sounds great when you're slouched on the sofa at home. Alternatively, you could come up with a concept – 1970s Eastern European disco, Californian folk music or early '80s new wave records made by people called Dave – and base your musical journey around that. There are no rules, so experiment and have fun.

Whatever you decide to do, make sure you prepare well beforehand. Take time selecting the records you want to put on the mix, and the sequence in which you'll play them. If there's plenty of beat matching involved (and there doesn't have to be – some of the best DJ mixes are simply blended), make sure you're comfortable with each individual mix before you start the recording. Once you've made the recording, listen back carefully; if you're not happy with the results, just do it again. This is your mix, after all, and you want it to be perfect.

WHAT YOU'LL NEED

First of all, you'll need something to record on to. Many DJs invest in a portable audio recorder. These are handheld devices designed to record audio to an SD or micro-SD flash memory card. To record DJ mixes, you'll need a model with an external line input

(quarter-inch jack, mini-jack or RCA phono, depending on the model) and the correct cable to connect it to the 'booth' or 'record' output on your mixer.

Alternatively, you could record directly to the hard drive of your laptop computer using free audio editing software, such as Audacity. Most laptops don't come bundled with audio line inputs, which means you may have to buy an external sound card. This sits between the mixer and laptop, with connections running in and out of the sound card. As with the portable recorder, ensure that you have the correct cables to connect everything together. Most external sound cards connect to a computer via USB.

← Ambient legend **Thomas Fehlmann of The Orb at his studio in Berlin.** He added samples of spoken word records, special effects and sounds of nature *(Rob Monk/ Future Music Magazine via Getty Images)*

Credit to the edit

What separates the greats of DJing from the rest of us isn't just their ability to entertain. Many devote their lives to preparing unique versions of tracks, known as re-edits.

You may be familiar with the idea of a 'remix'. For the uninformed, it's an interpretation of a song created using elements from the original recording and new musical features. In theory, remixes can be as radical as you want and contain only traces of the song being reinterpreted.

So what's a re-edit? As the name suggests, it's a re-arrangement of a song, edited to suit the needs of DJs. The first re-edits were created by New York disco DJs such as Danny Krivit, Walter Gibbons, Francois Kervorkian and Larry Levan in the late 1970s and early '80s. In those days, DJs created edits by cutting up reel-to-reel tape with the aid of a razor blade or scalpel, before carefully sticking the sections together with quarter-inch tape. It was a slow and laborious process even for the most skilful of editors.

Today, creating bespoke re-edits for your sets is a whole lot easier. These days, it can be done on a computer using free audio editing software. These programs allow you to view a song as a waveform display, so you can see the exact point where a new beat begins. Once you've selected a portion of audio, you can copy it, paste it into another point in the song, or even delete it altogether.

If you make your own re-edits, you'll always have something to play that nobody else has. You can also tailor your edits to suit the type of mixes you prefer. For example, many disco records can be hard to mix due to short drum breaks or loose drumming. You could 'fix' this by re-editing the track to include a longer, more stable drumbeat at the beginning and end.

That's not the only reason to get editing, either. Plenty of DJs have taken a mediocre track and turned it into dance floor gold, simply by removing the worst parts and emphasising the good bits. On other occasions, great edits have been made simply by allowing the groove a bit more time to work its magic, or restructuring a song so that it gradually builds towards a rousing finale.

Form and function

If you want to give re-editing a go, it pays to understand the structural rules of dance music. With one or two exceptions, musical elements or significant track changes always happen at predictable intervals. This is because dance music is made up of bars and phrases. There are four beats in a bar, 16 beats in a four-bar phrase and 32 beats in an eight-bar phrase. It is, of course, possible to use longer phrases (a 16-bar phrase of 64 beats, for example) but the music will end up sounding overly repetitive if subtle changes are few and far between.

If you're an avid music listener and DJ, this structural formula will already be hard-wired into your subconscious. Once you start re-editing, or making your own music, for that matter, you'll instinctively know when the track needs to change. By following your instincts and drawing on your own knowledge of what works on a dance floor, it shouldn't be long until you're creating rock-solid, club-friendly re-edits.

We can't finish this section without touching on the legalities of re-editing. Messing around with copyrighted musical material for your own pleasure – and DJ sets – is generally considered acceptable. If you leave it at that, you're not going to get any lawyers knocking at your door. However, if you make this music available to others, whether it's via the Internet or pressing up a box of white label records, then you could potentially be sued. You might not be, of course, but is it really worth the risk?

← Greg Wilson uses at least one reel-to-reel tape machine in each of his DJ sets. Before the advent of computer music production, DJs created their own edits by cutting and splicing reels of tape

Digital DJing

While this book is all about vinyl, you don't need decks and a mighty record collection to DJ in the 21st century. Here's a quick guide to the most popular methods of digital DJing…

If you've visited a club over the last decade, you may have noticed that the majority of DJs no longer use trusty old records and turntables. While traditional vinyl DJing has made a bit of a comeback in recent times, it remains largely the preserve of older DJs, dusty-fingered record collectors and those on the electronic music underground.

There are perfectly valid reasons to embrace digital DJing, though. If you own expensive, old or well-worn records, switching to digital music files or CDs could save them from excessive wear and tear. The additional functions available on modern digital DJing equipment also offer more opportunities for creative expression. Then there's portability; carrying a bag of 100 records

↓ High-profile DJs who do a lot of travelling often prefer to DJ digitally, as there's less stuff to cart around

makes little sense when you could turn up with two 64GB USB memory sticks packed full of WAV or 320 MP3 files.

Some vinyl DJs look down on those who choose to mix with music files and digital equipment. They point out that vinyl sounds better (which, on well-set-up and maintained sound systems, is true) and that DJing with records requires more skill. While there's merit in this argument – traditional turntables tend to drift out of time, whereas precise digital equipment doesn't – it seems a peculiar thing to get worked up about. After all, most listeners and dancers don't care whether you're playing a record, CD or MP3 file, just as long as it sounds good.

DJing digitally with your vinyl turntables

You don't have to ditch the decks completely to DJ digitally. You could purchase a Digital Vinyl System (DVS) such as Serato DJ (or its predecessor, Scratch Live) or Traktor Scratch Pro. As we briefly explained in Chapter 3, these systems allow DJs to mix music files stored on their computer, or a portable hard drive, using a regular set-up of two turntables and a mixer.

The software displays a graphical representation of each track on screen alongside other critical information, such as artist name, track title, tempo in BPM and time remaining. The software also boasts additional functions associated with digital DJing, such as the ability to create and save cue points (triggered by different key strokes), set up loops, use special effects or play back pre-recorded samples.

Using DJ controllers and DJing software

If you don't fancy vinyl-style mixing, many DJing software packages are now available. Some of these, such as PC DJ and Virtual DJ, are either relatively inexpensive or offer limited versions for free. All offer the ability to mix MP3 or WAV files using just your laptop computer, usually using the trackpad or mouse and various keyboard shortcuts. Some also boast 'sync' controls; enable this function and the software will mix the selected songs together automatically without you having to lift a finger.

It does take some of the fun out of DJing, but it's perfect if you're too lazy or drunk to mix.

Most digital DJs prefer a more 'hands-on' approach to mixing, so often connect a DJ controller to their laptop computer. As the name suggests, a DJ controller is a piece of equipment that features everything you need to perform a DJ set in one handy box. The layout and range of functions varies wildly between models, but all include everything you need to mix music, including a

↑ With a laptop, a DVS set-up and a hard drive containing thousands of tracks, it's possible to perform long sets without running out of music to play

← Standalone DJ controller units may look confusing and overloaded with features, but they're usually very easy to use

scaled-down DJ mixer. Some DJ controllers come bundled with a specific software application (Serato DJ, Traktor Scratch Pro and so on), while others can be used 'out of the box' without a connected laptop computer.

CD turntables and USB decks

By far and away the most popular digital DJing device is the CD turntable, though these days most are set up to also play music files stored on an external USB drive. Although many different models and makes are available, the 'industry standard' CD decks are those manufactured by Pioneer. The Japanese company revolutionised DJing when it released the CDJ-1000 at the dawn of the millennium, creating a digital turntable with a 'jog wheel' that could be manipulated in a similar way to records. Amazingly, it was even possible to perform scratches using the jog wheel's 'vinyl control' function.

Today, the CDJ-1000 has been superseded by the CDJ-2000 Nexus, a 'multi-player' turntable that allows DJs to mix digital music files (stored on a portable hard drive or flash memory drive) or CDs. DJs can now turn up to clubs with a pair of headphones and a couple of USB sticks and still be able to perform. CDJ-2000 units are very expensive, but cheaper Pioneer models using the same industry-standard control system are also available.

⬇ The world-famous Annie MacManus, aka Annie Mac, goes to work. Thanks to the USB capability of Pioneer's industry standard CDJ-2000s, most DJs now turn up to clubs with little more than a high-capacity portable flash drive and a pair of headphones

THE ANATOMY OF A CDJ-2000

① USB slot
Insert a USB flash drive or portable hard drive via USB and then press the 'USB' button to see the contents appear in the unit's graphical display. Tracks are selected using the control dial to the right of the display.

② SD card slot
Very few DJs actually use SD cards rather than USB drives, but Pioneer has included this option just in case you fancy giving it a go.

③ Loop controls
Use these to create your own loops in real time. They're a bit fiddly and take time to get used to, but with a bit of practice you'll soon be looping up sections of beats, music-free vocals and anything else that takes your fancy.

④ Jog wheel
In 'vinyl' mode, you can put your hands on this and scratch, or drop tracks into the mix, as you would on traditional turntables. You can also push and pull the sloped outer section of the platter to quickly speed up or slow down songs. In 'CDJ' mode, you can't scratch, but you can nudge the outer section with a light touch to perform minute timing adjustments.

⑤ Cue button
Use this to set a new start point for a track you wish to mix in. Press it after pausing a track during playback to set that as the new cue point.

6 **Link button**

When two or more CDJ-2000s are linked together via an Ethernet cable, it's possible to play tracks off a USB device plugged into either turntable. This is known as the 'link' mode.

7 **Display**

The top half shows the contents of any loaded USB stick, portable hard drive or MP3 CD loaded into the unit. The lower half shows current song information (beats per minute is on the far right of the screen) and, if you've used Pioneer's Rekordbox software to analyse and prepare beforehand, a waveform display. The software allows you to set and store loops and cue points. If you've done that, the points they appear in the song will also be shown.

8 **Jog mode**

This allows you to switch between two control methods: vinyl and CDJ. The former replicates the weight and feel of using DJ-friendly vinyl turntables.

9 **Tempo controls**

The tempo fader is used to slow down or speed up song playback, in a similar way to the pitch control feature on regular turntables. The tempo button allows you to change the BPM range. So, if you've ever wanted to slow down a really fast record so it sounds sludgy and demonic, now's your chance.

"It's reggae Time"

RECORDS

SOUL JAZZ RECORDS

100% DYNAMITE

2005 DYNAMITE SKA·SOUL·ROCKSTEADY

EPIC

ISLEY BROTHERS

FOREVER GOLD

Chapter Six

The vinyl resource

Essential accessories

As with all obsessions, record collectors can drain their bank accounts with accessories and add-ons. From record weights to crossfaders, here's your guide to the must-have vinyl kit.

'45' adaptors

Used to play 'dinked', jukebox-style 7in singles that boast a wider than normal centre hole, '45' adaptors are essential to DJs and record collectors alike. If you buy a brand-new turntable, it may come bundled with a cheap, plastic adaptor, but this kind has a tendency to get lost or broken. Because of this, we're big fans of weighty metal adaptors. There are loads of different designs available, so shop around.

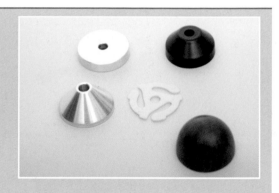

Record weights

The ultimate in audiophile DJ accessories, weights are designed to fit over the spindle and clamp a record in place. The idea is to ensure stability and guarantee better groove tracking during playback. They're particularly good for records that are lightly warped or misshaped. Various designs and weights are available, with the pricier offerings from boutique manufacturers proving popular.

(SoundFountain)

7in single slipmats

DJs often find mixing with 7in singles to be a pain in the backside, hence these selector-friendly slipmats. There are two types. The first are made from plastic, are 10in or 12in in diameter and feature a raised 7in-sized platter on which the record sits. Some also boast a built-in central adaptor for 'dinked' 45s. The second type is much simpler: a felt, 7in-sized baby slipmat for those dedicated to turntablist trickery.

Precision gauge

As any serious audiophile will tell you, it's imperative that your turntable is perfectly level. To that end, numerous brands offer a spirit gauge for those who want to cut down on unwanted deck sloping. Think of a precision gauge as a turntable-friendly spirit level, designed to neatly sit in the slot usually reserved for a '45' adaptor. They're relatively inexpensive and help cut down on uneven stylus wear.

(Audio Technica)

Isolation feet

Pop these underneath your turntable's usual feet to help cut down on unwanted vibrations, which can seriously impair sound quality. If your turntable is on the heavy side, select a stiffer set of isolation feet. If, on the other hand, your turntable is relatively lightweight, you'll need to opt for looser, more flexible feet.

(Audio Technica)

Contactless crossfader

The humble crossfader is the beating heart of any DJ mixer, so why not opt for a replacement fader that is guaranteed to last a lifetime? That's the bold claim behind the innovative, contactless InnoFader. The manufacturer claims that performance will remain constant over time thanks to its unique design. They're not cheap, but in our experience they're the best crossfaders out there.

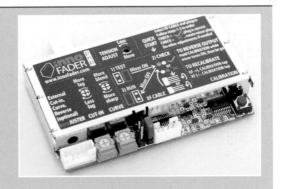

Stylus cleaner

We've previously talked about the importance of vinyl care, but it's vital to keep your 'needle' in good working order, too. To help ensure consistently high sound quality, you should clean the diamond tip of your stylus using a specialist brush and cleaning solution after every few plays, even if your records are in relatively good shape.

(turntableneedles.com)

Anti-static dust covers

It's a simple thing, but using proper 'inner sleeves' can really cut down on the amount of dust and grime that gets onto your records. There are three basic types: paper, plastic and poly-lined paper. Serious collectors tend to prefer the latter, as they not only protect the surface of the record, but also help to minimise the build-up of static during storage. You can often buy them in bulk from specialist online stores for very reasonable prices.

Portable crossfader

Turntablist DJs tend to be a little obsessed with scratching. Now they can scratch anytime, any place and anywhere thanks to the development of portable crossfaders. Combine one of these with a portable turntable – or even a smartphone – and you can cut and scratch music to your heart's content, regardless of whether or not you have a DJ mixer to hand.

Protective over-sleeves

If you've ever set foot in the record room of a serious collector, you may have noticed how most of their records sit inside plastic or PVC outer sleeves. These protect the record sleeves from wear and tear. Given that the condition of the sleeve has an impact on the value of a record, using this kind of precaution makes a lot of sense. There are many different types, weights and plastic materials to choose from, as well as variations to match different vinyl sizes (7in, 10in and so on).

Stylus pressure gauge

To cut down on needle and vinyl wear during playback, it's important to ensure that the downward pressure applied by your tonearm and needle – known as the 'tracking force' – is correct. The most accurate way to do this is by using a dedicated stylus or tracking force pressure gauge. Models vary from budget gadgets to expensive, high-precision implements.

(Ortofon)

Recycled vinyl eyewear

For the last few years, Vinylize designer Tipton Zachary has been making quality eyewear out of unwanted old records. His frames and sunglasses don't come cheap – think hundreds of pounds (or dollars) a pair – but they look fantastic and have proven popular with a number of well-known musicians. Presumably they don't warp or melt in the sun, unlike the records they're made of.

The best-selling LPs of all time

In 1981, worldwide sales of LPs touched one billion, including albums that became a staple of almost every collection. Here are the 25 most popular from the era when vinyl ruled the record stores.

Michael Jackson – Thriller (Epic, 1982)

Total certified sales: 46.3 million
Claimed total sales: 65 million

Assisted by a swathe of big-budget promotional videos and a swathe of superb songs, Michael Jackson's sixth solo album broke numerous records on its 1982 release. Following the singer's tragic death in 2009, it rocketed back up the album charts following incredible digital download sales. Sadly, no exact data is available for exactly how many copies *Thriller* has sold on wax, but it's rumoured to be well over 30 million – just under half of its claimed total sales.

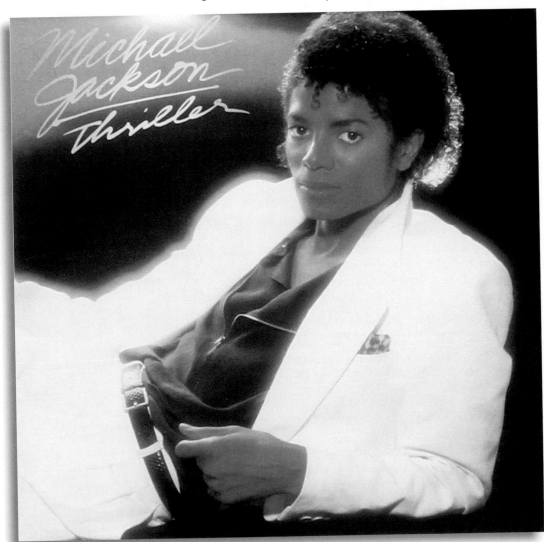

Eagles – Their Greatest Hits 1971–75 (Asylum, 1976)

Total certified sales: 32.2 million
Claimed total sales: 45 million

The Eagles' first 'best of' collection holds the honour of being the best-selling album of the 20th century in the United States. Weirdly, it doesn't contain some of their most

iconic material (the *Hotel California* album was released after this appeared in the shops), though it does boast such well-loved staples as 'Best of My Love' (later covered, bizarrely, by British reggae band Aswad) and 'One of These Nights'.

Led Zeppelin – Led Zeppelin IV (Atlantic, 1971)

Total certified sales: 29 million
Claimed total sales: 37 million

Jimmy Page, Robert Plant and company's fourth studio album has been named as the greatest rock album ever in numerous music magazine polls. It's certainly a brilliant set, even if it was responsible for introducing the world to 'Stairway To Heaven' – a song that pretty much every wannabe rock guitarist learns to play. We'll let you decide whether that's a good thing or not.

Fleetwood Mac – Rumours (Warner Brothers, 1977)

Total certified sales: 27.9 million
Claimed total sales: 40 million

Rumours may have been famously difficult to record – due, in part, to major fallings out between band members and their increasing reliance on cocaine – but it remains Fleetwood Mac's most glorious album. It's now such a part of our shared cultural heritage that most

people could recite the lyrics to a number of its songs. 'Dreams', in particular, is still a sing-along favourite. After three: 'Thunder only happens when it's raining…'

AC/DC – Back In Black (Atlantic, 1980)

Total certified sales: 26.1 million
Claimed total sales: 50 million

The Aussie hard-rockers reached their commercial peak with *Back In Black*, a long-player that included one of their most iconic songs, 'Hells Bells'. It also turned them into a major force in

the United States; to date, the set has sold over 23 million copies in North America.

Pink Floyd – The Dark Side of the Moon (Harvest, 1973)

Total certified sales: 24.2 million
Claimed total sales: 45 million

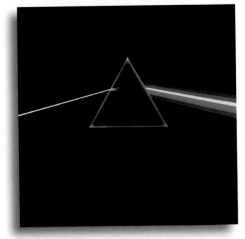

Almost everyone of a certain age owns a copy of *The Dark Side of the Moon* on vinyl, and possibly on CD, too. It's been reissued on wax numerous times in recent years, allowing a new generation to try syncing it up with 'The Wizard of Oz', as rather a large amount of people did (usually in various states of refreshment) during the 1970s. We've never tried, but apparently it does work if you get the timings exactly right.

Guns N' Roses – Appetite For Destruction (Geffen, 1987)

Total certified sales: 21.6 million
Claimed total sales: 30 million

When it first started appearing in record shops in the summer of 1987, Guns N' Roses' debut album largely sunk without trace. Amazingly, it took almost a year for the album to top the US Billboard chart; since then, it has notched up

over 140 weeks in the top 200. It turned Slash and Axl Rose into household names, capable of selling out huge stadiums across the world.

Meat Loaf – Bat Out of Hell (Epic, 1977)

Total certified sales: 21.5 million
Claimed total sales: 43 million

One of very few albums to have inspired a musical (it debuted in Manchester in early 2017 before transferring to London's West End), Meat Loaf's 1977 set is a theatrical, hard rock treat. At a time when pompous rock albums were all the

rage, *Bat Out of Hell* offered a perfect balance of heavy guitar riffs, overblown production and Meat Loaf's emotional vocals. The video produced to accompany the title track's single release hit a nerve with the public; we've lost count of the number of parodies we've seen over the years.

Eagles – Hotel California (Asylum, 1976)

Total certified sales: 21.5 million
Claimed total sales: 32 million

The Eagles arguably hit their creative peak with *Hotel California*, an LP described by

band member Don Henley as a concept album inspired by the state of the USA during its bicentennial year. Interestingly, album closer 'The Last Resort' mused on humanity's treatment of the environment, a theme that would become more common in music during the '80s and '90s (Sting, we're looking at you).

Michael Jackson – Bad (Epic, 1987)

Total certified sales: 21.3 million
Claimed total sales: 34 million

The King of Pop's follow-up to *Thriller* was big news in 1987. It flew off the shelves and continued to sell by the bucketload for years afterwards. Interestingly, it was the first album that

Jackson co-produced and boasted a string of iconic songs ('Smooth Criminal', 'The Way You Make Me Feel' and 'Man in the Mirror' being the best of the bunch).

The Bee Gees/Various Artists – Saturday Night Fever (Soundtrack) (RSO, 1977)

Total certified sales: 20.6 million
Claimed total sales: 40 million

In some ways, the *Saturday Night Fever* soundtrack – a lavish double-album featuring disco hits from the Bee Gees, the Trammps, Tavares and Kool & The

Gang, amongst others – is more significant than the film it was created for. It was the commercial zenith of the disco era. With rock fans fed up of mirror balls and John Travolta's white suit, the 'disco sucks' backlash began soon after the album's release.

Bruce Springsteen – Born in the U.S.A. (Columbia, 1984)

Total certified sales: 19.6 million
Claimed total sales: 30 million

The Boss was already big news before the release of *Born in the U.S.A.*, but the album turned him into a genuine global megastar. It was in his native America that the album naturally hit home hardest, though; to date, it has sold well over 15 million copies in the United States alone.

Various Artists – Dirty Dancing (Soundtrack) (RCA, 1987)

Total certified sales: 17.9 million
Claimed total sales: 32 million

Fittingly, the biggest-selling movie soundtrack of the 1980s was for one of the decade's most iconic films: Patrick Swayze/Jennifer Grey vehicle *Dirty Dancing*. The thing  is, can anyone remember any of the tracks other than Bill Medley and Jennifer Warnes' sing-along '(I've Had) The Time of My Life'? We suspect the answer is: no. Regardless, the album has notched up 11 platinum discs in the United States.

Whitney Houston – Whitney Houston (Arista, 1985)

Total certified sales: 17.9 million
Claimed total sales: 30 million

Whitney Houston may have ended up being a deeply troubled individual, but back in 1985 she was a fresh-faced soul singer with deep gospel roots. All that changed upon the release of her debut album, which included duets with legendary figures such as Jermaine Jackson and Teddy Pendergrass. A remixed version of the set, entitled *Dancin' Special*, was released in Japan (but, bizarrely, nowhere else) in 1986.

Bob Marley & The Wailers – Legend (Island, 1984)

Total certified sales: 13.47 million (US), 3.84 million (UK)
Claimed total sales: 25 million

If you were a student during the 1980s, it was likely that your small but compact record collection included a copy of *Legend*, the now ubiquitous Bob Marley & The Wailers 'best-of'.

It's the best-selling reggae album of all time worldwide, and continues to sell strongly on wax today thanks to numerous reissues. It was also remixed for re-release in 2013 by producers including Bob's son Ziggy Marley, dub legend Lee 'Scratch' Perry and drum & bass star Roni Size.

Dire Straits – Brothers In Arms (Vertigo, 1985)

Total certified sales: 17.7 million
Claimed total sales: 30 million

Despite vinyl still being the dominant format in 1985, *Brothers In Arms* was aimed at a growing breed of digital music buyers. It was one of the first sets to be recorded digitally (itself an expensive pursuit in those days) and the CD version went on to easily outsell its vinyl counterpart (despite there being both single and double-vinyl editions available). In many ways,

roll musical's 'OST' is one of the top five highest-selling soundtracks of all time. The album's best-known songs, 'You're The One That I Want', 'Summer Nights' and 'Greased Lightning', remain staples of wedding discos the world over.

it was the album that sped up the commercial demise of our beloved format. So, if anyone ever asks you who was responsible for the death of vinyl, blame Mark Knopfler.

Pink Floyd – The Wall (Harvest, 1979)

Total certified sales: 17.6 million
Claimed total sales: 30 million

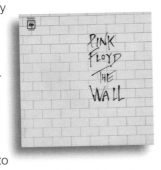

Pink Floyd's notably miserable rock opera about a reclusive singer is one of the biggest-selling double-albums of all time and Pink Floyd's most divisive full-length. According to the Recording Industry Association of America, it has sold in excess of 11 million copies on vinyl since its release at the tail end of 1979. It was later turned into a bizarre film starring Bob Geldof, featuring dystopian animations by original sleeve designer Gerald Scarfe.

Various Artists – Grease: The Original Soundtrack From The Motion Picture (RSO/Polydor, 1978)

Total certified sales: 14 million (US), 2.58 million (UK)
Claimed total sales: 28 million

Thanks to a lack of music industry record keeping between 1984 and 1991, it's hard to know exactly how many copies of this Olivia Newton-John and John Travolta-heavy soundtrack album were sold. We can say without any doubt, though, that the rock 'n'

The Beatles – Abbey Road (Apple, 1969)

Total certified sales: 14.4 million
Claimed total sales: 30 million

Despite containing the horror that is 'Maxwell's Silver Hammer', the Beatles' last hurrah (*Let It Be* was released later, but recorded earlier) remains one of their strongest albums. It famously boasts Ringo Starr's only drum solo (during his work with the Beatles, at least) and two of the most covered songs of all time (the George Harrison-penned 'Something' and 'Here Comes The Sun'). The album's iconic cover artwork also turned the zebra crossing outside Abbey Road studios in London into a tourist hotspot.

Phil Collins – No Jacket Required (Virgin, 1985)

Total certified sales: 12 million (US), 1.8 million (UK)
Claimed total sales: 25 million

Drummer-turned-solo artist Phil Collins hit the commercial heights with *No Jacket Required*, his third full-length outing. The album stayed at the top of the US album charts for seven straight weeks and went on to become one of the biggest sellers of the 1980s.

Interestingly, a number of tracks feature Collins on drum machine (rather than the standard drum set he usually used) and the back cover proudly proclaims: 'No Fairlights were used in the making of this record', a jokey reference to the pioneering Fairlight CMI music-making computer.

The Beatles – Sgt. Pepper's Lonely Hearts Club Band (Parlophone, 1967)

Total certified sales: 13.1 million
Claimed total sales: 32 million

The Fab Four's most iconic album celebrated its 50th birthday in the summer of 2017. It remains one of the most thrillingly imaginative and far-sighted albums of all time, as well as a brilliant advert for the creative potential of the recording studio (even if most Beatles scholars will tell you that *Revolver* is better). It could also be argued that it contains their single finest moment, 'A Day in the Life'. It has been claimed that the album has sold over 30 million copies, though only 13 million of those have been verified.

Bon Jovi – Slippery When Wet (Mercury/Vertigo, 1986)

Total certified sales: 12 million (US), 900,000 (UK)
Claimed total sales: 28 million

Given that it boasts two of Bon Jovi's best-loved songs – 'Livin' on a Prayer' and 'You Give Love a Bad Name' – it's perhaps unsurprising that *Slippery When Wet* is the hard rock/glam metal combo's most popular album. It

was an instant success when it was released in 1986 and helped Bon Jovi to become the first hard rock outfit to have two consecutive number one hit singles in the United States.

Simon & Garfunkel – Bridge Over Troubled Water (Columbia, 1970)

Total certified sales: 8 million (US), 3.2 million (UK)
Claimed total sales: 25 million

Paul Simon and Art Garfunkel's final studio album remains a high-water mark in folk-rock. Simon was at his lyrical best on tracks such as 'The Boxer' and 'The Only Living Boy in New York', while the album's production was staggeringly good. While Paul Simon would later go on to create a string of well-regarded and commercially successful albums – think *Graceland* and *Rhythm of the Saints*, in particular – Art Garfunkel has struggled to reach similarly dizzy heights.

Madonna – Like a Virgin (Sire, 1984)

Total certified sales: 10 million (US), 900,000 (UK)
Claimed total sales: 25 million

Although Madonna's 1983 debut album offered a superb, radio-friendly distillation of the latest New York dance trends (assisted, in no small part, by a cast of supporting characters

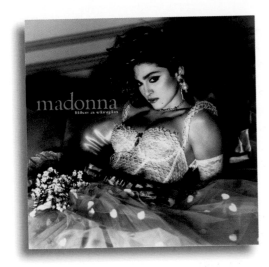

including leading underground remixers Mark Kamins and then boyfriend John 'Jellybean' Benitez), it was her 1984 follow-up that's the better pop record. Buoyed by production from Chic's Nile Rodgers and a string of hit singles ('Material Girl' and 'Like a Virgin' included), the album propelled Madonna further towards global superstar status.

Carole King – Tapestry (Ode, 1971)

Total verified sales: 10 million (US)
Claimed total sales: 25 million

One of the more surprising entries in this list, Carole King's *Tapestry* managed both critical and commercial success following its release in 1971. The album earned King a swathe of Grammy Awards in 1972, including Best Album. Finding exact sales figures for territories outside the US has proven tricky, though we do know that the 1991 CD reissue has sold over one million copies in Japan.

SILVER, GOLD AND PLATINUM DISCS

Over the years, music industry bodies have handed out awards to artists who achieve major sales milestones. The exact list of awards and sales required to achieve them varies from country to country, but are normally 'silver', 'gold' and 'platinum' discs. If you sell over 10 million copies of an album or single in the United States, you're awarded a rare 'diamond disc'. The awards and the sales they represent are as follows:

United States of America
Gold Disc: 500,000 copies (album or single)
Platinum Disc: 1 million copies (album or single)
Diamond Disc: 10 million copies (album or single)

United Kingdom
Silver Disc: 60,000 (album) / 200,000 (single)
Gold Disc: 100,000 (album) / 400,000 (single)
Platinum Disc: 300,000 (album) / 600,000 (single)

The best-selling singles of all time

There was a time when countries held their breath to find out what song was topping the singles charts, with an amazing 550 million sales a year at their peak. These are the ultimate sellers.

Bing Crosby – 'White Christmas' (Decca, 1942)

Total physical units sold: 50 million

When the first *Guinness Book of Records* was published in 1955, it proudly proclaimed Bing Crosby's 'White Christmas' – first released as a 78rpm, 10in shellac single during the Second World War – to be the highest-selling song of all time. According to the most recent edition of the trivia bible, the song has now topped 100 million in sales if digital download sales, compilation appearances and Internet streams are taken into account. Roughly half of the total sales cited by the record keepers at Guinness were on physical formats, most notably vinyl.

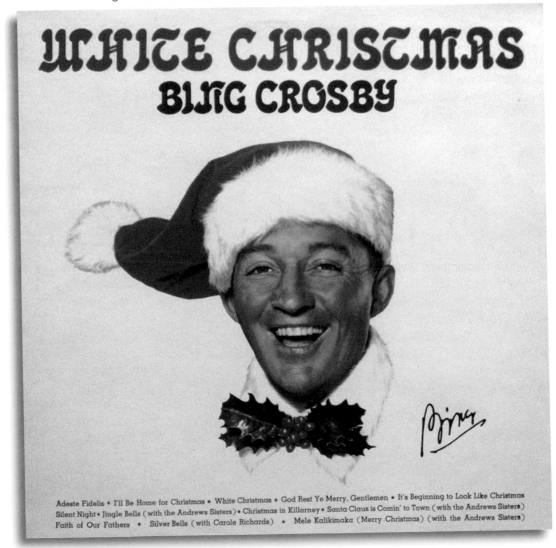

Bing Crosby – 'Silent Night'
(Decca, 1942)

Total physical units sold: 30 million

Crosby first unveiled his cover version of traditional Christmas favourite 'Silent Night' on a 1940 compilation of yuletide music. It was reissued several times as a single throughout the 1940s and '50s, racking up sizeable sales in the process. While nowhere near as popular as 'White Christmas', it remains a staple of Christmas compilations, alongside Crosby's unlikely 1977 collaboration with David Bowie ('Peace On Earth/Little Drummer Boy') and various Christmas songs recorded by Nat 'King' Cole.

Mungo Jerry – 'In The Summertime'
(Dawn, 1970)

Total physical units sold: 30 million

With nine UK top-ten singles to their name, Mungo Jerry can hardly be classed as one-hit wonders. Even so, 'In The Summertime' remains the only Mungo Jerry song that anyone remembers. Given that it topped the charts all over the world in 1970 (aside from the US, where it reached number three on the Billboard Top 100) and has so far sold over 30 million copies, that's probably not that surprising. The least said about Shaggy's largely forgotten 1995 cover version, the better.

Bill Haley & His Comets – 'Rock Around the Clock' (Decca, 1954)

Total physical units sold: 25 million

Few singles have been quite as influential as Bill Haley & His Comets' version of 'Rock Around the Clock'. Although it wasn't the first rock 'n' roll record, it helped to popularise the style worldwide. Interestingly, it sold relatively poorly

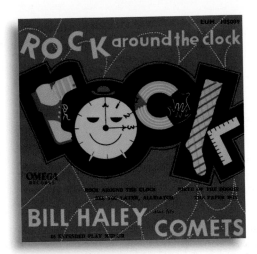

on its original 1954 release, and only rocketed to the top of the US and UK charts following its inclusion in the opening credits of rebellious 1955 film *Blackboard Jungle*.

Domenico Mudungo – 'Nel blu dipinto di blu (Volare)'
(Fomit Centra/Decca, 1958)

Total physical units sold: 22 million

You may not know 'Volare', as it is popularly known, by name, but there's a fair chance you would recognise it if you heard it. The biggest-selling non-English language single of all time, the song was initially recorded by Italian singer Domenico Mudungo in 1958 and was chosen as Italy's entry to that year's Eurovision Song Contest. It topped the charts in the United States and in recent years has formed the basis of a number of popular football terrace chants.

Elvis Presley – 'It's Now Or Never'
(RCA Victor, 1960)

Total physical units sold: 20 million

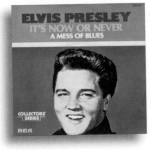

Elvis's best-selling single, 'It's Now Or Never', was based on an earlier Italian song, the 1898 composition 'O Sole Mio'. Presley had the idea of creating his own version of the song after hearing Tommy Martin's 1949 interpretation of the Italian classic, 'There's No Tomorrow', while serving in the US Army. After topping the US charts, demand in the UK was high, but rights issues forced the release to be delayed. When it eventually appeared in stores, it spent eight weeks at number one.

USA For Africa – 'We Are The World' (CBS, 1985)

Total physical units sold: 20 million

America's answer to Band Aid, United Support of Artists for Africa was the brainchild of Harry Belafonte, fundraiser Ken Kragen, and writers Michael Jackson and Lionel Richie. Like the UK single that inspired it, 'We Are The World' was recorded in one session, where producer Quincy Jones was joined by a cast-list of big-ticket musicians, including Bruce Springsteen, Bob Dylan, Stevie Wonder, Paul Simon, Diana Ross, Willie Nelson, most of the Jackson family and, in a nod to the song that inspired it, Bob Geldof.

The Ink Spots – 'If I Didn't Care' (Decca, 1939)

Total physical units sold: 19 million

Arguably one of the first global pop hits, 'If I Didn't Care' has all but been forgotten in recent years. Historically, it's rather important, though. The group who popularised it, The Ink Spots, were one of the first acts to cross America's race divide, with both white and black listeners responding to their trademark blend of barbershop, easy listening and what would later be dubbed rhythm and blues. Curiously, 'If I Didn't Care' never made it to the top of the sales charts, though five of their other 1939 singles did achieve number one status.

John Travolta & Olivia Newton-John – 'You're The One That I Want' (RSO, 1978)

Total physical units sold: 15 million

Such was the popularity of John Travolta and Olivia Newton-John's duet that it topped the UK singles chart before the movie it was taken from, *Grease*, had even opened in cinemas. It stayed at the top of the British charts for nine weeks in the summer of 1978. Interestingly, another song from the rock 'n' roll musical, 'Summer Nights', also spent seven weeks at number one in the autumn of '78. Sadly, Travolta's solo follow-up, the dreadful disco single 'A Girl Like You', didn't fare so well.

Kaoma – 'Lambada' (CBS, 1989)

Total physical units sold: 15 million

In the steamy summer of 1989, we all went a little 'Lambada' crazy. The song (and accompanying dance craze) helped make superstars of French band Kaoma, for a few months at least. The single – a jaunty, accordion-heavy chunk of Latin dance-pop – didn't make that much of a splash in the United States, though it did top the charts in France (where it stayed for 12 weeks, notching up nearly two million sales) and ten other countries. Kaoma were later successfully sued for sneakily translating an earlier Bolivian song without permission. Oops.

Bryan Adams – '(Everything I Do) I Do It For You' (A&M, 1991)

Total physical units sold: 15 million

In 1991, Bryan Adams' sickly-sweet power ballad dominated the UK singles chart to such an extent that it stayed at number one for a record-breaking 16 weeks. The song achieved similarly impressive sales figures in the United States and Adams' native Canada. Sales were no doubt helped by the song's appearance in one of 1991's

most commercially successful movies, *Robin Hood: Prince of Thieves*, which featured Kevin Costner's mullet in the title role.

Gloria Gaynor – 'I Will Survive'
(Polydor, 1978)

Total physical units sold: 14 million

Gloria Gaynor's anthem to female empowerment may now be more associated with drunken wedding discos, but it remains one of the most popular

dance anthems of all time. Originally, the song appeared on the B-side of Gaynor's cover of The Righteous Brothers' 'Substitute', but there was little appetite for that amongst club and radio DJs. Instead, they championed the superior B-side. Gaynor's label, Polydor, quickly reversed the sides and reissued it. The rest, as they say, is history.

Scorpions – 'Wind of Change'
(Vertigo/Mercury, 1991)

Total physical units sold: 14 million

German hard rock band the Scorpions were inspired to write 'Wind of Change', a power ballad commenting on the fall of communism in Eastern Europe, following a concert in

Moscow in 1989. The record naturally struck a chord not only in their native Germany, where it is still considered an anthem of re-unification, but also elsewhere across the world. The Scorpions were certainly thankful to the Soviets

for the inspiration; later in 1991, they presented a gold disc to peacemaking President Mikhail Gorbachev.

Kyu Sakamoto – 'Sukiyaki'
(Toshiba/EMI, 1961)

Total physical units sold: 13 million

When EMI decided to issue Kyu Sakamoto's hit in English-speaking countries, they ignored the translation of the song's actual title ('I Look Up As I Walk')

and named it after a Japanese beef stew instead. Whether this helped or hindered the marketing is unclear, but the song remains the only Japanese language record ever to top the US singles charts. If you've not heard it, the song is worth a listen; it sounds remarkably like American easy listening from the rock 'n' roll era.

Trio – 'Da Da Da' (Mercury, 1982)

Total physical units sold: 13 million

As part of the *Neue Deutsche Welle* movement, Trio were committed to making their songs as simple and repetitive as possible. On 'Da Da Da', they

took this approach to its logical conclusion, delivering a song built around a mere three guitar chords, sparse electronic drums and a mantra-like, nonsensical vocal. Much to their surprise, it became a big hit in Germany, so they re-recorded it in English. Predictably, the Anglicised version went on to become a smash all over the world.

Gene Autrey – 'Rudolph The Red-Nosed Reindeer' (Columbia, 1949)

Total physical units sold: 12.5 million

In 1939, US department store chain Montgomery Ward published a festive booklet by writer Robert L. May telling the story of 'Santa's ninth reindeer'. Over the next decade, the chain handed out millions of copies, inspiring May's brother-in-law, Johnny Marks, to turn it into a song. In 1949, Gene Autry was recruited to sing it, and his

recording sold 1.75 million copies en route to becoming the Christmas number one. If you add in sales of all later cover versions, the song has sold almost 150 million records in total.

The Beatles – 'I Want To Hold Your Hand' (Parlophone, 1963)

Total physical units sold: 12 million

The Beatles' follow-up to 'She Loves You' had already racked up pre-orders of over a million copies in the UK before it even hit record stores. When it

was eventually released in the United States in February 1964, promoted by the Beatles' now infamous appearance on the *Ed Sullivan Show*, 'Beatlemania' swept the country. The song remains the Fab Four's best-selling single, ahead of epic sing-along 'Hey Jude', which has so far sold an impressive eight million copies.

Village People – 'Y.M.C.A.' (Casablanca, 1978)

Total physical units sold: 12 million

The Young Men's Christian Association took a dim view of the Village People's infamous disco tribute to their community centres. Although the band's lead

singer and lyricist, Victor Willis, has claimed that the song was an innocent celebration of the organisation's role in offering activities for inner-city kids, the YMCA feared that it was

really about young homosexual men 'cruising' for partners. In the end, the two sides settled out of court and the Village People scored their biggest global hit.

Band Aid – 'Do They Know It's Christmas?' (Phonogram/Columbia, 1984)

Total physical units sold: 12 million

It was 25 November, 1984, when Midge Ure and Bob Geldof gathered together some of the UK's biggest pop stars – and, bizarrely, US disco outfit Kool & The Gang

– to record a festive-themed charity single. The record was made in a day, rush-released and sold in staggering numbers in the weeks that followed, earning millions of pounds for charities working to fight famine in Ethiopia. The success of the record paved the way for 1985's Live Aid concerts and a number of successful re-recordings.

Carl Douglas – 'Kung Fu Fighting' (Pye/20th Century Fox, 1974)

Total physical units sold: 11 million

According to legend, 'Kung Fu Fighting' was made in two takes at the end of a recording session. The producer, Biddu Appiah, had intended it to be a

B-side, but Carl Douglas's label, Pye, had other ideas. They made the novelty disco record, which was partly inspired by the popularity of kung-fu movies, the A-side. In hindsight, it was a smart move: the record topped the charts on both sides of the Atlantic and ended up selling over 11 million copies in total.

George McRae – 'Rock Your Baby' (TK Records, 1973)

Total physical units sold: 11 million

If 'Kung-Fu Fighting' helped to popularise disco, it could be argued that 'Rock Your Baby' was responsible for defining the style in the public's imagination. The influence of McRae's dance floor classic can be heard in everything from ABBA's 'Dancing Queen' to, more surprisingly, John Lennon's 'Whatever Gets You Through The Night'. It was also one of the first hit singles to make use of a drum machine, then something of a novelty.

The Mills Brothers – 'Paper Doll' (Decca, 1943)

Total physical units sold: 11 million

Songwriter Johnny S. Black didn't live to see 'Paper Doll', a song he wrote in 1915, become one of the best-selling records of all time. He passed away in 1936, seven years before The Mills Brothers' recording became the United States' most in-demand single. The song spent 12 weeks at the top of the Billboard chart from November 1943 onwards, becoming one of the biggest sellers of the pre-rock 'n' roll era.

Roger Whittaker – 'The Last Farewell' (RCA, 1971)

Total physical units sold: 11 million

When Roger Whittaker invited listeners to his British radio show to submit their own poems, which he would then set to music, he had no idea what he'd let himself in for. Amongst the million or so replies he received was a poem by a Birmingham silversmith named Ron Webster. Whittaker recorded his version of Webster's 'The Last Farewell' in 1971, but it took four years to become a hit single on both sides of the Atlantic.

ABBA – 'Fernando' (Polar Music, 1976)

Total physical units sold: 10 million

It's something of a surprise to find that ABBA's biggest-selling single is not 'Waterloo' or 'Dancing Queen', but their heartfelt ballad about a man who has lost his greatest love. Band member Anni-Frid Lyngstad originally recorded it in Swedish for her 1975 solo album *Frida Ensam*, before ABBA produced their own version with altered English lyrics. It became the biggest single of 1976, selling some six million copies in that calendar year alone.

Roy Acuff & His Crazy Tennesseeans – 'Wabash Cannon Ball' (Okeh, 1938)

Total physical units sold: 10 million

Written sometime in the late 19th century, American railroad folk song 'Wabash Cannon Ball' was a popular staple in the early part of the 20th century. Country music pioneers The Carter Family released the first notable version in 1932, before singer Roy Acuff put out his own take in 1938. Sales rocketed over the years that followed, peaking in 1942. Such was the popularity of the record during and after the Second World War that it eventually notched up sales in excess of 10 million.

THE 10-MILLION CLUB

Fewer than 40 singles have ever sold more than 10 million units worldwide. Those not included in our countdown include a trio of huge hits from the era of CD singles: Elton John's tribute to Diana, Princess of Wales, 'Candle In The Wind 1997' (33 million units sold), Celine Dion's 'My Heart Will Go On' (also 1997, 15 million units sold) and Whitney Houston's 'I Will Always Love You', which sold a staggering 20 million copies. Other notable 10-million sellers include Elvis Presley's 'Hound Dog', Britney Spears's '...Baby One More Time' and the Monkees' 'I'm A Believer'.

The A–Z of music on vinyl

Don't go crate digging until you know your House from your Hip Hop to your Metal. This guide will help you to spot the diamonds in the rough.

Ambient

What is it? Laid-back, often beatless music that emphasises tone and texture in order to deliver atmospheric sounds. Ambient music was pioneered by the likes of Brian Eno and Robert Fripp in the 1970s, enjoyed an electronic revival in the '90s thanks to artists such as The Orb and Aphex Twin, and is now undergoing a surge in popularity in the 21st century.

Sub-genres: Ambient House, Ambient Dub, Ambient Techno, New Age.

Must-have records: Brian Eno – *Ambient 1: Music For Airports* (EG, 1978), Jon Hassell & Brian Eno – *Fourth World, Vol. 1: Possible Musics* (Editions EG, 1980), The KLF – *Chill Out* (KLF Communications, 1990), The Orb – *Adventures Beyond The Ultraworld* (Big Life, 1991), Aphex Twin – *Selected Ambient Works Volume 1* (Apollo/R&S Records, 1992), The Higher Intelligence Agency & Pete Namlook – *S.H.A.D.O EP* (Fax, 1997), Gaussian Curve – *Clouds* (Music From Memory, 2014).

Sought-after obscurities: The KLF – *Madrugada Eterna* (12in test pressing, 1990). Only a handful of white label test pressings of this ambient house classic exist, plus later counterfeit 'bootleg' white labels.

Trivia: In the 1990s, Paul McCartney dabbled in ambient music with producer Youth (aka former Killing Joke member Martin Glover) as The Fireman.

Bass music

What is it? A 'catch all' term applied to bass-heavy dance music, mostly by lazy journalists.

In this context, it applies to dubstep, grime, UK garage and other dance floor variants of those styles. All of these combine elements of other types of electronic dance music with the weighty basslines associated with Jamaican soundsystem culture. Many of the earliest dubstep records were pressed up in very limited quantities on white label 12in singles, making them expensive collectors' items amongst 'bassheads' and dance music historians.

Sub-genres: Breakstep, Dubstep, Grime, UK Garage, 8-Bar.

Must-have records: Dem 2 – *Destiny* (Locked On, 1997), Wookie – *Wookie* (S2S, 2000), MJ Cole – *Sincere* (Talkin' Loud, 2000), Maddslinky – *Reject/Desert Fog* (Sirkus, 2001), Horsepower Productions – *In Fine Style* (Tempa, 2002), Burial – *Burial* (Hyperdub, 2006), Pinch – *Underwater Dancehall* (Tectonic, 2007), Digital Mystikz – *Return II Space* (DMZ, 2010).

Sought-after obscurities: Any of the early releases on pioneering dubstep label DMZ will set you back serious money, especially 2004's *Twisup / B* 12in by Loefah and Digital Mystikz.

Trivia: UK garage initially developed when a small group of London DJs combined sped-up US garage records with the weighty basslines of drum & bass.

Classic rock

What is it? Rock music from the style's 'golden age' in the 1960s, '70s and '80s, including material by many of the most iconic artists of all time. Classic rock collectors tend

to focus on obscure or limited-edition records by many of the artists, rather than their popular works.

Sub-genres: None (aside from the various sub-genres that different classic rock records fall into).

Must-have records: The Beatles – *Revolver* (Parlophone, 1966), Cream – *Disraeli Gears* (Reaction, 1967), The Jimi Hendrix Experience – *Are You Experienced* (Track Records, 1967), The Band – *Music From Big Pink* (Capitol Records, 1968), Led Zeppelin – *II* (Atlantic, 1979), The Rolling Stones – *Exile On Main Street* (Rolling Stones Records, 1972), Aerosmith – *Toys In The Attic* (Columbia, 1975), David Bowie – *The Rise & Fall Of Ziggy Stardust & The Spiders From Mars* (RCA Victor, 1972).

Sought-after obscurities: Few Beatles collectors could afford to buy a copy of the exceedingly rare 'butcher cover' version of US compilation *Yesterday & Today*, so-called because it features the Fab Four fondling bits of dead animal. The last copy to go on sale fetched in the region of £11,500 ($15,000)!

Trivia: In 1969 just 200 copies of the Rolling Stones' *Promotional Album* (snappy title, lads) were pressed and sent to radio stations. A pristine copy will now set you back thousands of pounds.

Classical music

What is it? Timeless music composed at various points over the last 1,000 years, but mostly used to refer to works that have been performed since the latter half of the 18th century. Although new classical works are still being composed, it's often interpretations of older pieces that get classical music buffs hot under the collar. When it comes to collecting classical music, the devil's in the detail: serious collectors focus on particular conductors, orchestras and recordings, rather than specific composers, symphonies or concertos.

Sub-genres: Early Music, Baroque, Opera, Expressionism, Modernism, Neo-Classical, Minimalism.

Must-have records: Victor De Sabata & Teatro Alla Scala – *Puccini: Tosca* (EMI Classics, 1953), Evgeny Mravinsky & The Leningrad Philharmonic Orchestra – *Tchaikovsky: Symphony No. 6* (Deutsche Gramaphon, 1957), George Solti & The Vienna Philharmonic Orchestra – *Wagner: Das Rheingold & Die Walkure* (Decca, 1960), Daniel Barenboim & The English Chamber Orchestra – *Mozart: Piano Concertos No. 20/No. 23* (His Master's Voice, 1967), Carlos Kleiber & The Wiener Philharmoniker – *Beethoven: Symphonie No. 5* (Deutsche Gramaphon, 1975), Steve Reich – *Music For 18 Musicians* (ECM, 1978).

Sought-after obscurities: According to *Record Collector* magazine, rare records by acclaimed classical soloists are amongst the most in-demand. A good example is Gioconda De Vito's 1957 recording of Bach's 'Violin Concerto in E Major' on His Master's Voice.

Trivia: Arguably the most famous classical composition of the last 70 years is John Cage's '4'33', a 'three act' performance that requires performers not to touch their instruments at all. Yep, that's four minutes, 33 seconds of silence.

Country

What is it? The sound of the south of the USA, country music is still regarded as being 'the voice of working-class America'. Country songs can usually be divided into

two distinct groups: those designed for dancing along to, and heart felt ballads. It's the latter style that has served many greats of the style – think Tammy Wynette and Johnny Cash, for starters – so well over the last 60 years.

Sub-genres: Bluegrass, Bakersfield Sound, Nashville Sound, Western Swing, Honky Tonk, Outlaw Country, Red Dirt.

Must-have records: The Carter Family – *The Carter Family Album* (Liberty, 1962), Patsy Cline – *Sentimentally Yours* (Decca, 1962), Luke The Drifter (aka Hank Williams, Snr) – *Movin' On* (MGM, 1966), Johnny Cash – *At Folsom Prison* (Columbia, 1968), Tammy Wynette – *Stand By Your Man* (Epic, 1969), David Allen Coe – *The Mysterious Rhinestone Cowboy* (Columbia, 1974), Waylon Jennings, Willie Nelson, Jessi Colter & Tompall Glaser – *Wanted: The Outlaws* (RCA, 1976), Dolly Parton, Linda Ronstadt & Emmylou Harris – *Trio* (Warner Brothers, 1987), Clint Black – *Killin' Time* (RCA, 1989).

Sought-after obscurities: According to the experts at Vinylbeat, the most valuable country album is Jim Reeves' 1955 set *Jim Reeves Sings on Abbot*, which will set you back around £780 ($1,000) – assuming, of course, you can find a copy.

Trivia: Before the 'country music' tag became popular in the 1940s, many referred to the style as 'hillbilly music'.

Disco

What is it? The dominant style of dance floor soul music in the mid to late 1970s, disco was arguably the first style of music to be tailored specifically to the needs of dancers. Disco labels pioneered remix culture by asking leading DJs to create extended club mixes, which were than pressed onto 12in singles. Despite the style's commercial success, it remains popular with collectors, who naturally gravitate towards the obscure and little known.

Sub-genres: Dub Disco, Italo-Disco, Disco-Funk, Boogie, Electrofunk, Synth Disco, AOR Disco, Euro-Disco, Nu-Disco.

Must-have records: MFSB – *Love Is The Message* (Philadelphia International, 1973), Sylvester – *You Make Me Feel (Mighty Real)* (Fantasy, 1978), Loleatta Holloway – *Love Sensation* (Gold Mind/Salsoul, 1980), D-Train – *You're The One For Me* (Prelude, 1981), Logg – *Logg* (Salsoul, 1981), North End – *Happy Days* (Emergency, 1981), Taana Gardner – *Heartbeat* (West End, 1981), Chaka Khan – *I Feel For You* (Warner Brothers, 1984).

Sought-after obscurities: There are plenty of disco records with an eye-watering price tag, though few are quite as expensive as the rarely seen 12in version of Mistafide's little-known disco-rap joint 'Equidity Funk'. It changes hands online for thousands.

Trivia: The first commercially available 12in single was Double Exposure's 1976 single, 'Ten Percent', on Salsoul Records. It featured a ten-minute club version by leading New York DJ, Walter Gibbons.

Drum & Bass

What is it? The genre formerly known as jungle, famed for sped-up breakbeats, heavyweight basslines and high-speed MC mic chatter. The earliest jungle records, which largely drew influence from dub, reggae and ragga, emerged out of the UK hardcore scene around 1992–93. Since then, drum & bass has gone on to be one of the most popular styles of dance music worldwide, with a younger generation of DJs now paying close attention to the earliest records. Traditionally, D&B artists and labels have championed vinyl over digital formats, with many top selectors even pressing up their own exclusive, one-off 'dubplates' of unreleased tunes.

Sub-genres: Jungle, Liquid Funk, Darkstep, Techstep, Jump-Up, Neurofunk.

Must-have records: Goldie – *Timeless* (1995), Origin Unknown – *The Speed of Sound* (Ram, 1996), Various – *LTJ Bukem Presents Earth Volume 1* (Earth, 1996), Roni Size/Reprazent – *New Forms* (Talkin' Loud, 1997), Peshay – *Miles From Home* (Blue, 1998), Aphrodite – *Aphrodite* (V2, 1999), Photek – *Solaris* (Science/Virgin,

2000), High Contrast – *True Colours* (Hospital, 2002).

Sought-after obscurities: In 1995, seminal label Moving Shadow created a special ten-disc set of their *Two On One* compilation series, housed in a Pizza Hut takeaway box. Around 30 were created and given to label artists. On the rare occasions copies come up for sale, they go for around £400 ($520).

Trivia: British mic man Rebel MC is thought to have first popularised the term 'jungle' while rapping at hardcore raves.

Electronica

What is it? Technically, any music made with computers and electronic instruments, though 'electronica' is usually used to describe electronic music of a more experimental nature. Collectors tend  to look for both hard-to-find rarities from popular artists – think Kraftwerk, Aphex Twin, Autechre, Boards of Canada and the like – as well as deliciously strange, pioneering records made by trailblazing experimentalists of the late 1960s and early '70s.

Sub-genres: Intelligent Dance Music (IDM), Folktronica, Jazztronica, Breakcore.

Must-have records: BBC Radiophonic Workshop – *BBC Radiophonic Music* (BBC Records, 1968), Tangerine Dream – *Electronic Meditation* (Ohr, 1970), Kraftwerk – *Autobahn* (Philips, 1974), Throbbing Gristle – *20 Jazz Funk Greats* (Industrial, 1979), Yellow Magic Orchestra – *Technodelic* (Alpha, 1981), Arthur Russell – *World of Echo* (Upside/Rough Trade, 1986), Various Artists – *Artificial Intelligence* (Warp Records, 1992), Radiohead – *OK Computer* (Parlophone, 1997), Boards of Canada – *Music Has The Right To Children* (Warp, 1998).

Sought-after obscurities: Many keen collectors look for obscure albums of electronic 'library music' from the early days of the style. As these were never commercially released, finding them can be tricky. Many of the finest examples, such as Chappell's 1973 effort by The Machines, *Electronic Music*,

fetch significant sums of money on the rare occasions that they come up for sale online.

Trivia: Beatles member George Harrison was an early advocate for electronic music. He released an album of his own experiments, entitled *Electronic Sound*, in 1969.

Folk

What is it? Strictly speaking, it's the music of the people. 20th- and 21st-century folk is inspired by traditional music that dates back centuries. Many of these Celtic and  English traditions were in danger of dying out before the infamous 'folk revival' that gathered pace in the 1960s. Keen collectors are always on the lookout for obscure albums and singles pressed up in small quantities, as well as rarities from heavyweights of the '60s scene such as Bob Dylan, Leonard Cohen, Joni Mitchell and Judy Collins.

Sub-genres: Folk-rock, Folktronica, Folk Blues, Electric Folk, American Primitivism.

Must-have albums: The Weavers – *The Weavers At Carnegie Hall* (Vanguard, 1957), Woody Guthrie – *Dust Bowl Ballads* (Folkways, 1964), Bob Dylan – *The Times They Are A-Changin'* (Columbia, 1964), Paul Simon – *The Paul Simon Songbook* (CBS, 1965), Leonard Cohen – *Songs of Leonard Cohen* (Columbia, 1967), Sandy Denny – *Sandy* (Island, 1972), John Martyn – *Solid Air* (Island, 1973), Richard & Linda Thompson – *I Want To See The Bright Lights Tonight* (Island, 1974).

Sought-after obscurities: Look no further than the rare first stereo pressing of Bob Dylan's 1963 album *The Freewheelin' Bob Dylan*, which contained four tracks deleted from subsequent versions. A mint copy once fetched an astonishing £27,000 ($35,000) at auction.

Trivia: Paul Simon famously wrote 'Homeward Bound' while waiting at Widnes railway station in Cheshire, England, in 1975.

Hip hop

What is it? An entire sub-culture incorporating rap music, outlandish DJ techniques, break dancing and graffiti. What started with DJs playing records in the backstreet parks and recreation centres in the Bronx, New York, is now one of the world's most popular forms of musical entertainment.

Sub-genres: Gangsta Rap, Glitch-Hop, Trip-Hop, Crunk, R&B, Miami Bass, Experimental Hip Hop.

Must-have records: Run-DMC – *Run-DMC* (Profile, 1984), N.W.A. – *Straight Outta Compton* (Ruthless, 1988), Public Enemy – *It Takes A Nation of Millions To Hold Us Back* (Def Jam, 1988), Beastie Boys – *Paul's Boutique* (Capitol Records, 1989), De La Soul – *3 Feet High & Rising* (Tommy Boy, 1989), A Tribe Called Quest – *The Low-End Theory* (Jive, 1991), Dr. Dre – *The Chronic* (Interscope, 1992), The Wu-Tang Clan – *Enter The Wu-Tang (36 Chambers)* (RCA, 1993), 2Pac – *All Eyez On Me* (Interscope/Death Row, 1996), Mos Def – *Black On Both Sides* (Rawkus, 1999).

Sought-after obscurities: The ultimate hip-hop collector's item is undoubtedly Wu-Tang Clan's 2014 album *Once Upon A Time In Shaolin*. Just one copy exists, and was sold to a private collector via auction for £1.5 million ($2 million).

Trivia: Many critics have argued that the first rap record ever recorded was the Last Poets' eponymous debut album, which hit stores in 1970. It featured members of the collective speaking rhythmically over freestyle jazz music.

House

What is it? The dominant force in dance music since the middle of the 1980s, house was born in the underground clubs of Chicago. Initially, it sounded like

stripped-back disco with drum machines, but it has since moved in a multitude of different directions. Collectors tend to focus on obscure records pressed in limited numbers, rather than the well-known anthems heard in clubs.

Sub-genres: Acid House, Deep House, Tech-House, Progressive House, Ambient House, Hip-House, EDM, Soulful House.

Must-have records: Frankie Knuckles – *Baby Wants To Ride/Your Love* (TRAX, 1987), Phuture – *Acid Trax* (TRAX, 1987), A Guy Called Gerald – *Voodoo Ray* (Rham!, 1988), Mr Fingers – *Ammnesia* [sic] (Jack Trax, 1989), St Germain – *Boulevard (The Complete Series)* (F Communications, 1995), Daft Punk – *Homework* (Virgin, 1996), Moodymann – *Silentintroduction* (Planet E, 1997).

Sought-after obscurities: The first Alleviated Records pressing of Mr Fingers' pioneering 1985 Chicago deep house cut 'Mystery Of Love' rarely comes up for sale. Far easier to find is the 1986 DJ International version, credited to Fingers Inc, and featuring different mixes.

Trivia: There have been many arguments over the years about who made the first ever house record. According to most dance music historians, the prize goes to Chicago DJ Jesse Saunders, whose track 'On & On' was released at the tail end of 1984.

Indie

What is it? The term 'indie' was originally used to describe music that was released by independent record labels (as opposed to the 'major labels' such as EMI and Universal), but these

days it's applied mainly to 'indie pop' and 'indie rock' acts. Indie music, as we know it today, first became popular during the 1980s, when a string of bands and artists signed to independent labels topped the albums and singles charts. Since then, many top 'indie' acts have gone on to sign for major labels.

Sub-genres: Indie-rock, Indie-pop, Britpop, Grunge, Emo, Shoegaze, Math Rock.

Must-have records: The Smiths – *The Queen Is Dead* (Rough Trade, 1986), Sonic Youth – *Daydream Nation* (Enigma/Blast First, 1988), Nirvana – *Bleach* (Sub-Pop, 1989), Pixies – *Doolittle* (4AD, 1989), Primal Scream – *Screamadelica* (Creation, 1991), Blur – *Modern Life Is Rubbish* (Food, 1993), Pulp – *His 'N' Hers* (Island, 1994), Weezer – *Weezer* (DGC,

1994), Oasis – *(What's The Story) Morning Glory?* (Creation, 1995).

Sought-after obscurities: A handful of 7in test pressings of the Smiths' debut single, 'Hand In Glove', were produced in 1983. Industry bible *Record Collector* values these at a whopping £1,800 apiece.

Trivia: The cover of Blur's 1994 album *Parklife* features photographs taken at Walthamstow Stadium in the East End of London. The greyhound-racing venue hosted its final race in August 2008, 75 years after it first opened.

Jazz

What is it? Arguably the most revolutionary form of 20th-century popular music, jazz is known for musical improvisation, unique time signatures and its enduring influence on  many other styles of music. With over a century of releases to choose from, plus a myriad of sub-genres, jazz collectors won't run out of records to hunt down. For this reason, some collectors choose to focus on specific variations or particular artists.

Sub-genres: Free-Jazz, Spiritual Jazz, Jazz Fusion, Jazz-Funk, Afro-Jazz, Latin Jazz, Modal, Be-bop, Hard-bop, Soul-Jazz, Swing.

Must-have records: Billie Holliday – *Billie Holliday At Jazz At The Philharmonic* (Clef, 1954), Duke Ellington & The Buck Clayton All-Stars – *At Newport* (Columbia, 1956), Ella Fitzgerald – *Ella Fitzgerald Sings The Cole Porter Songbook* (Verve, 1957), Miles Davis – *Kind of Blue* (Columbia, 1959), Charles Mingus – *Mingus Ah Um* (Columbia, 1959), Ornette Colman – *Free Jazz* (Atlantic, 1960), John Coltrane – *A Love Supreme* (Impulse, 1964), Herbie Hancock – *Head Hunters* (Columbia, 1973), Sun Ra – *Space Is The Place* (Blue Thumb, 1973), Weather Report – *Heavy Weather* (Columbia, 1976), Pat Metheny Group – *Still Life (Talking)* (Geffen, 1987).

Sought-after obscurities: In 2015, a pristine copy of Hank Mobley's eponymous 1957 album on Blue Note was sold online for well over £7,000 ($9,000).

Trivia: The London Jazz Collector website estimates that there are only around 200 'high-end' record collectors around the world chasing the most valuable jazz releases. If you're thinking of becoming the 201st, you'll need deep pockets.

Metal

What is it? The loudest music known to mankind, full of layered, ludicrously noisy guitar riffs and screamed vocals. Metal has its roots in the heavy rock movement of the late 1960s and early 70s (think Black Sabbath, Deep Purple, Judas Priest and Motorhead), before becoming a stadium-filling phenomenon in the 1980s. Amongst the most collectable of sub-genres is black metal, a style pioneered in the 1980s and made popular by Norwegian bands in the 1990s.

Sub-genres: Black Metal, Death Metal, Nu-Metal, Grindcore, Alternative Metal, Extreme Metal.

Must-have records: Black Sabbath – *Master of Reality* (Vertigo, 1971), Motorhead – *Ace Of Spades* (Bronze, 1980), Judas Priest – *British Steel* (Columbia, 1980), Iron Maiden – *The Number of the Beast* (EMI, 1982), Metallica – *Master of Puppets* (Elektra, 1986), Slayer – *Reign In Blood* (Def Jam, 1986), Megadeth – *Rust In Peace* (Capitol, 1990), Rage Against The Machine – *Rage Against The Machine* (Epic, 1992).

Sought-after obscurities: A copy of Mayhem's obscure 1987 black metal 12in, *Deathcrush*, sold online in January 2017 for just shy of £1,500. Bizarrely, it features a cover of a track written by German experimental electronica composer Conrad Schnitzler.

Trivia: There is much debate about the origins of the term 'heavy metal'. The term was first used in song by Steppenwolf on the 1968 classic 'Born to Be Wild', but wasn't used to describe hard rock music until the early 1970s. It's likely it caught on after appearing in reviews by journalists Lester Bangs and Mike Saunders in 1968 and '71 respectively.

Pop

What is it? Popular music, of course! Unlike other styles of contemporary music, pop has the loosest definition of all. Great pop records can mine almost any genre you can think of, as long as they're addictive, easy to listen to and sound great on the radio. Because pop releases are aimed at becoming huge chart hits, record labels normally throw huge marketing budgets at them. That means lots of special promotional items, limited edition releases and endless 12in singles containing club-friendly extended versions. Favoured artists of pop collectors include Madonna, the Pet Shop Boys, Prince, David Bowie and, of course, the Beatles.

Sub-genres: Art-pop, Synth-pop, Europop, K-Pop, J-Pop, Bubblegum Pop.

Must-have records: The Beach Boys – *Pet Sounds* (Capitol, 1966), The Beatles – *Sgt Pepper's Lonely Hearts Club Band* (Parlophone, 1967), ABBA – *Arrival* (Polar, 1976), Michael Jackson – *Thriller* (Epic, 1982), Madonna – *Like A Virgin* (Sire, 1984), Peter Gabriel – *So* (Charisma, 1986), Pet Shop Boys – *Actually* (Parlophone, 1987), Prince – *Sign O' The Times* (Paisley Park, 1987), Spice Girls – *Spice* (Virgin, 1996), Lady Gaga – *The Fame Monster* (Streamline, 2009).

Sought-after obscurities: The 12in picture-disc edition of Madonna's 'Erotica' single was withdrawn from sale shortly after it arrived in shops back in 1992. These days, a copy would set you back a couple of thousand pounds (or dollars, for that matter).

Trivia: According to academic research, the term 'pop song' was being used as far back as 1926 to describe 'music with popular appeal'.

Progressive rock

What is it? Rock music that takes risks. The arty, mind-altering style first emerged on the back of the psychedelic movement of the late 1960s, going on to reach the peak of its commercial powers in the 1970s. Progressive rock bands favoured concept albums (the stranger the better), long tracks, musical elements borrowed from classical and jazz, and lyrical references to wizards. Oh, and rock operas on ice.

Sub-genres: Art-rock, Krautrock, Post-rock, Symphonic rock, Neo-progressive rock.

Must-have records: King Crimson – *In The Court of the Crimson King* (Island Records, 1971), Yes – *Fragile* (Atlantic, 1971), Jethro Tull – *Aqualung* (Chrysalis, 1971), Genesis – *Foxtrot* (Charisma, 1972), Emerson, Lake & Palmer – *Emerson, Lake & Palmer* (Island, 1970), Mike Oldfield – *Tubular Bells* (Virgin, 1973), Rush – *212* (Mercury, 1976), Pink Floyd – *Animals* (Harvest, 1977), The Alan Parsons Project – *Eye In The Sky* (Arista, 1972).

Sought-after obscurities: Until the 1990s, few people even knew of the existence of Northampton prog band Dark. Only 64 copies of their 1972 debut album, *Around The Edges*, were initially pressed. Twelve of these have full-colour gatefold sleeves and will set you back serious money. Happily, it has been reissued numerous times since the 1990s.

Trivia: The term 'progressive rock' was first coined to describe radio stations that played underground rock music, rather than a particular style of music.

Punk

What is it? A thrilling, no holds barred, two-fingered salute to the music industry. When it emerged in the US and UK in the mid-1970s, punk was a grassroots revolt against the worst excesses of the music industry. For years, punk thrived on a 'do-it-yourself' ethos that encouraged its participants to press up their own records. As a result, the style is rich pickings for collectors.

Sub-genres: Post-punk, Punk-funk, Mutant Disco, Skate Punk, Punk-pop, Hardcore punk, Art-punk.

Must-have records: Ramones – *Ramones* (Sire, 1976), The Clash – *The Clash* (CBS, 1977), Television – *Marquee Moon* (Elektra, 1977), Wire – *Pink Flag* (Harvest, 1977), Buzzcocks – *Another Music In A Different Kitchen* (United Artists, 1978), Black Flag – *Damaged* (Unicorn, 1981), Crass – *Penis Envy* (Crass Records, 1981), Descendents – *Milo Goes To College* (New Alliance, 1982), Sonic Youth – *Evol* (SST, 1986), Green Day – *Dookie* (Reprise, 1994).

Sought-after obscurities: The A&M Records 7in single edition of the Sex Pistols' 1977 anthem 'God Save The Queen' was withdrawn before it hit the shops. It's rumoured that only 300 are in circulation, hence a seriously high price tag (especially if it's accompanied by the record label's original press release).

Trivia: The first wave of punk acts was hugely influenced by earlier US garage-rock acts such as The Stooges and MC5.

Reggae

What is it? Jamaica's finest musical export has been popular across the world, particularly in the UK, the US and Japan, since the 1960s. Reggae collectors have a multitude of sub-

genres and related styles to explore, as well as decades worth of small-run, Jamaican-made 7in singles to track down. The collecting scene is naturally centred on specialist record dealers, though rare items do come up for sale online from time to time.

Sub-genres: Ska, Roots, Rocksteady, Lovers Rock, Dub, Ragga, Dancehall.

Must-have records: The Maytals – *Never Grow Old* (Studio One, 1963), Horace Andy – *Skylarking* (Studio One, 1972), Various – *The*

Harder They Come (Island, 1972), Upsetters – *14 Dub Blackboard Jungle* (Upsetter, 1973), Bob Marley & The Wailers – *Catch A Fire* (Island, 1973), Augutus Pablo – *East of the River Nile* (Message, 1978), Scientist – *Scientist Meets The Space Invaders* (Greensleeves, 1981), Yellowman – *Mister Yellowman* (Greensleeves, 1982), Gregory Isaacs – *Night Nurse* (Island, 1982), Mad Professor – *Dub Me Crazy Part 5: Who Knows The Secret Of The Master Tape?* (Ariwa, 1985).

Sought-after obscurities: 1961's *All Star Top Hits*, a ska compilation album on Coxsone Records (reissued later the same year on UK imprint Blue Beat) is rarely seen for sale and has long been a 'holy grail' of many reggae collectors.

Trivia: The first record to explicitly mention reggae as a musical description is thought to be Toots & The Maytals' 1968 single 'Do The Reggay'.

Soul & Funk

What is it? Radio-friendly dance music that emerged out of black American communities in the early 1960s. Thanks to the success of record labels such as Stax, Motown and Atlantic,

soul and funk artists found global fame from the mid-1960s onwards. Many later movements, such as disco, have their roots in soul. Both styles have long been popular with record collectors, especially 'Northern Soul', a style built around record collecting one-upmanship. Rare 7in soul singles can fetch eye-watering prices when they come up for sale.

Sub-genres: Neo-Soul, Hip-hop Soul, Disco, Boogie, Quiet Storm, Blue-eyed Soul, Deep Funk, Go-go, P-funk.

Must-have records: James Brown – *Live at the Apollo* (King, 1963), Sam Cooke – *Ain't That Good News* (RCA, 1964), Otis Redding – *Otis Blue/Otis Redding Sings Soul* (Volt, 1965), The Supremes – *I Hear a Symphony* (Motown, 1966), Aretha Franklin – *I Never Loved A Man The Way That I Love You* (Atlantic, 1967), Dusty Springfield – *Dusty In Memphis* (Atlantic,

1969), Sly & The Family Stone – *There's A Riot Goin' On* (Epic, 1971), Marvin Gaye – *What's Going On?* (Tamla, 1971), Stevie Wonder – *Innervisions* (Tamla, 1973), Parliament – *Mothership Connection* (Casablanca, 1975).

Sought-after obscurity: In 2009, one of the only two known copies of Frank Wilson's 1965 single 'Do I Love You (Indeed I Do)' sold for an astonishing £25,000 ($33,000). Even copies of the more widely available 1979 Tamla-Motown UK reissue will set you back upwards of £60.

Trivia: Although 'Northern Soul' is now an accepted name for a certain style of driving 1960s soul music, mostly from the Detroit area, the term was initially used to refer to the type of records played in specialist northern English clubs in the 1960s and '70s.

Techno

What is it? Futurist electronic dance music, originally from the Motor City of Detroit, but now made throughout the world. The original techno pioneers, the so-called 'Belleville

Three' of Juan Atkins, Derrick May and Kevin Saunderson, were hugely inspired by science fiction and the possibilities of space travel. Since the 1980s, the style has mutated into a myriad of forms, some of which are unrecognisable from the trio's original blueprint. Many underground techno records are pressed in small quantities, guaranteeing high second-hand prices for the most sought-after items.

Sub-genres: Minimal Techno, Tech-house, Dub Techno, Intelligent Techno, Acid Techno.

Must-have records: Model 500 – *Sound of Stereo/Off To Battle* (Metroplex, 1986), Rythim Is Rythim – *Nude Photo* (Transmat, 1987), Reese – *Just Want Another Chance* (Incognito, 1988), Joey Beltram – *Energy Flash* (Transmat, 1990), LFO – *LFO* (Warp, 1990), Maurizio – *Ploy* (Maurizio, 1992), Galaxy 2 Galaxy – *Galaxy 2 Galaxy* (Underground Resistance, 1993), The Black Dog – *Temple of Transparent Balls* (GPR, 1993), Plastikman – *Spastik* (NovaMute, 1993), Ricardo Villalobos – *Fizheuer Zieheur* (Playhouse, 2006).

Sought-after obscurities: Look no further than the record that started it all: Model 500's 'No UFOs'. The original 1985 pressing on Metroplex still commands a sizeable price tag, despite numerous reissues.

Trivia: Ten Records' 1988 compilation album, *Techno! The New Dance Sound of Detroit*, was the first release to refer to the music as 'techno'.

World Music

What is it? The term 'world music' gained popularity in the 1980s, primarily as a term to describe records made by artists from non-English-speaking countries. It's an umbrella term that covers a huge number of different musical styles from Africa, Asia, South America and the Far East. Records from countries that don't have a particularly established music industry tend to be those that collectors flock to, as they're generally incredibly hard to find. Many collectors choose to focus on particular countries or styles (Brazilian samba or Nigerian synth-pop, to give two examples).

Sub-genres: Some of the most popular with collectors include Afrobeat, Qawwali, Highlife, Samba, Tango, Mbaqanga, Flamenco, Makossa, Mambo, Raga, Balkan Beat and Gypsy Jazz.

Must-have records: Tito Puente – *Pachanga Con Puente* (Tico, 1961), Fela Ransome Kuti & Africa '70 – *Expensive Shit* (Soundworkshop, 1975), King Sunny Ade & His African Beats – *Juju Music* (Sunny Alade, 1982), Ofra Haza – *Yemenite Songs* (Hed-Arzi, 1984), Astor Piazzolla – *Tango: Zero Hour* (American Clave, 1987), Nusrat Fateh Ali Khan – *Musst Musst* (Real World, 1990), Orchestra Baobab – *Pirates Choice* (World Circuit, 1989), Salif Keita – *Amen* (Mango, 1991), Buena Vista Social Club – *Buena Vista Social Club* (World Circuit, 1997).

Sought-after obscurities: A copy of Peter Abdul's 1984 Nigerian boogie album *Get Down With Me* changed hands on Discogs Marketplace in December 2016 for almost £1,000 ($1,300).

Further reading

BOOKS

Matt Anniss, *DJing for Beginners* (Amber Books, 2016)

Bill Brewster & Frank Broughton, *How To DJ Properly* (Bantam Press, 2002)

Bill Brewster & Frank Broughton, *Last Night a DJ Saved My Life* (Headline, 2000)

Bill Brewster & Frank Broughton, *The Record Players* (Virgin Books, 2012)

John Corbett, *Vinyl Freak: Love Letters to a Dying Medium* (Duke University Press, 2017)

Mike Evans, *Vinyl: The Art of Making Records* (Sterling, 2015)

Frank Hoffman, *Encyclopedia of Recorded Sound* (Routledge, 2004)

Bernd Jonkmans, *Record Stores: A Tribute to Record Stores* (Seltmann, 2015)

Andy McDuff & Ian Shirley, *Record Collector: The Rare Record Price Guide 2016* (Metropolis Business Publishing, 2014)

Brett Milano, *Vinyl Junkies: Adventures in Record Collecting* (St Martin's Press, 2003)

Jenna Miles, *The Beginner's Guide to Vinyl: How to Build, Maintain and Experience a Music Collection in Analog* (Adams Media Corporation, 2016)

Mike Morsch, *The Vinyl Dialogues: Stories Behind Memorable Albums of the 1970s As Told by the Artists* (Biblio Publishing, 2014)

Tim Neely, *Goldmine Price Guide to 45rpm Records* (KP Books, 2009)

Michael Ochs, *1000 Record Covers* (Taschen, 2014)

Joaquim Paulo & Julius Widdemann, *Jazz Covers* (Taschen, 2015)

Eilon Paz & RZA, *Dust & Grooves: Adventures in Record Collecting* (Top Speed Press, 2015)

Amanda Petrusich, *Do Not Sell at Any Price: The Wild, Obsessive Hunt for the World's Rarest 78rpm Records* (Scribner, 2015)

Josh Rosenthal, *The Record Store of the Mind* (Tompkins Square Books, 2015)

Courtney E. Smith, *Record Collecting For Girls: Unleashing Your Inner Music Nerd, One Album at a Time* (Mariner Books, 2011)

Mike Spitz & Rebecca Vilaneda, *The Record Store Book: 50 Legendary and Iconic Places to Discover New and Used Vinyl* (Rare Bird Books, 2015)

Dave Thompson, *Goldmine Jazz Album Price Guide* [Third Edition] (Krause Publications, 2016)

Dave Thompson, *Goldmine Record Album Price Guide* [Eighth Edition] (Krause Publications, 2015)

Dave Thompson, *The Music Lover's Guide to Record Collecting* (Backbeat Books, 2002)

Paul E. Winters, *Vinyl Records and Analog Culture in the Digital Age: Pressing Matters* (Lexington Books, 2016)

WEBSITES

Audio Technica: www.audio-technica.com

Bozak: www.bozak.com

Claremont 56: www.claremont56.bandcamp.com

Collectors Frenzy: www.collectorsfrenzy.com

Discogs: www.discogs.com

GZ Vinyl: www.gzvinyl.com

IDJ: www.internationaldjmag.com

Juno Records: www.juno.co.uk

Long Live Vinyl magazine: www.anthem-publishing.com/longlivevinyl

LoveVinyl: www.lovevinyl.london

Optimum Mastering: www.optimum-mastering.com

Popsike: www.popsike.com

Record Collector Magazine: www.recordcollectormag.com

Richer Sounds: www.richersounds.com

Scratch Pro Audio: www.scratchproaudio.co.uk

Sugarbush Records: www.sugarbushrecords.com

Vinyl Factory: www.thevinylfactory.com/

What Hi-Fi?: www.whathifi.com

Index